GRADUATES

DISCOVERING YOUR DESTINY...

GOD'S
WAY

WHITE STONE BOOKS

LAKELAND, FLORIDA

07 06 05 04   10 9 8 7 6 5 4 3 2 1

GRADUATES—DISCOVERING YOUR DESTINY...GOD'S WAY
ISBN 1-59379-015-5
COPYRIGHT © JOHN M. THURBER
THURBER CREATIVE SERVICES, INC.
TULSA, OKLAHOMA

EDITORIAL DEVELOPMENT AND LITERARY REPRESENTATION BY
MARK GILROY COMMUNICATIONS, INC.
6528 E. 101ST STREET, SUITE 416
TULSA, OKLAHOMA 74133-6754

PUBLISHED BY WHITE STONE BOOKS
P.O.BOX 2835
LAKELAND, FLORIDA 33806

introduction

God is faithfully at work today in the lives of people around the world—revealing His purpose, demonstrating His awesome power, and transforming lives into incredible futures.

Maybe you are looking for answers on how to successfully navigate the next few years of your life.

Perhaps you need a little inspiration to help you tackle head on a brand new path. Maybe you are looking at continuing your education, or even securing your first "real" job.

God's Way for Graduates is filled with true-life stories that reveal powerful insights from individuals experiencing the same range of life situations as you; true-life stories from people who have looked to God for help and inspiration—and received it.

Discover the incredible potential and excellence God has appointed for your life as you continue on your life's journey—and seek to achieve what it truly means to live…*God's Way.*

contents

GRADUATES

DISCOVERING YOUR DESTINY...

GOD'S WAY

kudos for kelsey

LANITA BRADLEY BOYD

If I ride the wings of the morning, if I dwell

by the farthest oceans, even there your hand will

guide me, and your strength will support me.

PSALM 139:9-10 NLT

Kelsey's high school graduation day! I was as excited as she was. Graduation, however, paled in comparison to the other events of the day. We were eagerly looking forward to two very special guests who would be attending the graduation exercises and celebrating with us afterward.

An arriving flight from Amarillo to Cincinnati was bringing in our guests and only one hour before graduation. My husband, Steve, really wanted to be the first to greet them, so he went to the airport alone. We had asked our good friend Terri to be our backup, and Steve would call her to pick them up for us if the plane was late. We didn't want to risk being late for our only daughter's graduation!

All went well. Steve recognized them from their pictures and met them with open arms. The three were enwrapped in a huge hug until Steve finally took a step back.

"Patty, I've wanted to say this for 18 years: I just want you to know how much I appreciate your willingness to let us have Kelsey. I simply want to thank you for the joy and blessing that she has been to our lives."

Patty hardly knew what to say. "I'm honored to be here," she responded. "Kelsey is a precious young lady. You all have done a great job with her."

On the ride to our home, Steve talked with Patty and Kevin about Kelsey's visit to them during her spring break that year. "It was an amazing time for all three of us," Kevin said. "When the social worker called and said that our daughter was searching for us and wanted to make contact, I was completely overwhelmed. I think I had both feared and longed for the day we would get that call. But it all worked out really well."

Steve said, "How do you want to be introduced to people this weekend? I want you to be as comfortable as possible here."

"Just as friends," Patty said quickly. "I don't want to be labeled as 'the birthmother' that 'gave up' this beautiful child."

"No problem!" Steve answered. But in the flurry of their hurried arrival at our home and rushing to the high school, there was no time for Steve to relay the conversation to me.

As we entered the lobby, my friend Sally, who had also been Kelsey's English teacher, came hurrying up to Patty and me. "Oh, good, you made it! Here are your tickets. The four of you are right down front." She paused, looking expectantly at Patty.

"Sally, this is Patty Duke, Kelsey's birthmother," I said. Unlike Steve, until that moment I had given no thought as to how I would introduce Patty.

As Sally took her hand, Patty seemed to stiffen a bit. Quickly I explained to Patty, "Sally teaches here now, but she is also a lawyer. In fact, she is the lawyer who handled the adoption for us. She's been in on this from the beginning!"

Patty smiled and relaxed. I made a mental note to introduce her as Patty from Amarillo from then on. Steve and Kevin found us, and we went to our seats without fanfare.

The graduates filed in to "Pomp and Circumstance" and my eyes welled. *How could eighteen years have passed so quickly? How could this lovely woman beside me have signed over that beautiful baby girl to total strangers? Why were we so blessed?*

As the ceremonies proceeded, I was lost in thought about the way God had worked to bring this child to our family. Patty had left her New Mexico college campus to go to Denver to have a baby without the knowledge of her parents. Our friend in Memphis had put us in touch with the Denver adoption agency that Patty found in the yellow pages. All these years she had assumed her daughter was living in Denver and we had in turn assumed Kelsey's birthmother lived in Denver!

At age eighteen, as we had planned together, Kelsey began searching for her birthmother through the adoption agency. But Patty had come with a bonus: Kevin. When the social worker told us that Patty was married to Kelsey's birthfather, we were astonished. They had married six years after Kelsey was born.

And now here we sat, the four of us, listening to the principal talk about what a solemn occasion this was and how for the sake of time we would have no applause for each graduate. An obedient group, we sat as each name was decorously announced and the student crossed the stage to receive the appropriate diploma.

Just as Kelsey's name was called and she started across the stage, the woman beside me erupted. "Yea, Kelsey!" she yelled, clapping vigorously with Kevin joining her. "Way to go!"

Kelsey, blushing, took her seat, but I could tell she was pleased. She had always felt special because of Patty's decision eighteen years earlier. Knowing how reserved Patty usually was, she again felt blessed upon hearing Patty's overt show of pride. This was not a day when Kelsey had had to blend in with the crowd.

Kelsey is confident that God brought her to us and then brought Patty and Kevin to her. She sees her destiny in His hands and is willing to go where He sends her. So far, through our family, that has ranged from Nashville, Tennessee, to Brazil, to Cincinnati, Ohio, and to Thailand, teaching the good news of Jesus Christ.

Now Kelsey has also graduated from college, again with Patty and Kevin's love, support, and attendance. She is getting a graduate degree to teach English as a second language, either in the United States or abroad. She is eagerly watching and ready for what's next in God's great plan for her life.

smiley

KAREN MAJORIS-GARRISON

Freely you have received, freely give.

MATTHEW 10:8 NIV

I was in the prima donna, self-centered age of seventeen, and my motives were simple—to enhance my final grade in Health Assistant class. To accomplish this goal, I decided to volunteer at the nearby convalescent center.

For weeks I grumbled to my boyfriend. "I can't believe I'm stuck taking care of old people for free!" He agreed. The bright yellow uniforms my classmates and I were required to wear made matters even worse. On our first day at the center, the nurses took one look at our sunshiny apparel and nicknamed us "The Yellow Birds."

During my scheduled days, I complained to the other "yellow birds" how emptying bedpans, changing soiled linens, and spoon-feeding pureed foods to mumbling mouths were not jobs any teenager should have to do.

A tedious month passed, and then I met Lily. I was given a tray of food and told to take it to her room. Her bright blue eyes appraised me as I entered, and I soon became aware of the kindness that rested behind them. After talking with her for a few minutes, I realized why I hadn't noticed Lily before, although I had been past her room numerous times. Lily, unlike so many of the other residents, was soft-spoken and undemanding. My first day at the convalescent home, I discovered the staff had their favorite patients—usually those with character that stood out in some way. From joke-tellers to singers, the louder and more rambunctious the patient, the more attention they received.

Something inside of me immediately liked Lily, and strangely, I even began to enjoy our talks during my visits to her room. It didn't take long for me to realize that Lily's genuine kindness stemmed from her relationship with God.

"Come here," she said and smiled to me one rainy afternoon. "Sit down. I have something to show you." She lifted a small photo album and began to turn the pages. "This was my Albert. See him there? Such a handsome man." Her voice softened even more as she pointed to a pretty, little girl sitting on top of a fence. "And that was our darling Emmy when she was eight years old."

A drop of wetness splattered on the plastic cover, and I quickly turned to Lily. Her eyes were filled with tears. "What is it?" I whispered, covering her hand with my own.

She didn't answer right away, but as she turned the pages I noticed that Emmy was not in any other photographs. "She died from cancer that year," Lily told me. "She'd been in and out of hospitals most of her life, but that year she went home to Jesus."

"I'm so sorry," I said.

"It's okay," she smiled slightly, meeting my eyes. "God is good to those who love Him, and He has a plan for every life, Karen. We need to open our hearts to Him whether we understand His ways or not. Only then can we find true peace." She turned to the last page. Inside the worn album was one more picture of a middle-aged Lily standing on tiptoes and kissing a clown's cheek.

"That's my Albert," she laughed, recalling happier memories. "After Emmy died, we decided to do something to help the children at the hospitals. We'd been so disturbed by the dismal surroundings while Emmy was hospitalized." Lily went on to explain how Albert decided to become "Smiley the Clown."

"Emmy was always smiling, even in the worst of times. So I scraped together what fabric I could find and sewed this costume for Albert." She clasped her hands in joy. "The children loved it! Every weekend, we volunteered at the hospitals to bring smiles and gifts to the children."

"But you were so poor! How did you manage that?" I asked in amazement.

"Well," she grinned, "smiles are *free,* and the gifts weren't anything fancy." She closed the album and leaned back against her pillows. "Sometimes the local bakers donated goodies, or when we were really hurting for money, we'd take a litter of pups from our farm. The children loved petting them. After Albert died, I noticed how faded and worn the costume was, so I rented one and dressed as Smiley myself; that is...until my first heart attack, about ten years ago."

When I left Lily's room that day, I couldn't think of anything other than how generous she and Albert had been to children who weren't even their own.

Graduation day neared, and on my last day of volunteer services at the ward, I hurried to Lily's room. She was asleep, curled into a fetal position from stomach discomfort. I stroked her brow, worrying about who would care for her the way I did. She didn't have any family, and most of the staff neglected her except for her basic needs, which were met with polite abruptness. At times, I wanted to proclaim Lily's virtues to the staff, but she'd stop me, reminding me that the good things she'd done in life were done without thoughts of self. "Besides," she would say, "doesn't the good Lord tell us to store our treasures in heaven and not on this earth?"

Lily must have sensed my inner torment above her bed that day as she opened her eyes and touched my hand. "What is it, dear?" she asked, her voice concerned and laced with pain.

"I'll be back in two weeks," I told her, explaining about my high-school graduation. "And then I'll visit you every day. I promise."

She sighed and squeezed my fingers. "I can't wait for you to tell me all about it."

Two weeks later, I rushed back to the center, bubbling with excitement and anxious to share with Lily the news of my graduation events. With a bouquet of lilies in my hand, I stepped into her clean, neat, but unoccupied room. The bed was made, and as I searched for an answer to Lily's whereabouts, my heart already knew the answer.

I threw the flowers on the bed and wept.

A nurse gently touched my shoulder. "Were you one of the yellow birds?" she asked. "Is your name Karen?" I nodded, and she handed me a gift-wrapped box. "Lily wanted you to have this. We've had it since she died because we didn't know how to get in touch with you."

It was her photo album. Written on the inside cover was the scripture Jeremiah 29:11: "For I know the plans I have for you," declares the LORD, "plans to prosper you and not to harm you, plans to give you hope and a future." I clutched it to my chest and departed.

Three weeks later, my horrified boyfriend stood before me. "You can't be serious!" he said, pacing back and forth. "You look ridiculous."

We were in my bedroom, and as I tried to view myself in the mirror, he blocked my reflection. "You can't be serious," he repeated. "How in the world did you pay for that thing anyway?"

"With my graduation money," I answered.

"Your what?" he exclaimed, shaking his head. "You spent the money that we saved for New York on *that?*"

"Yep," I replied, stringing on my rubber nose. "Life should be more about giving than receiving."

"This is just great," he muttered, helping me tie the back of the costume. "And what am I supposed to tell someone when they ask me my girlfriend's name? That it's Bozo?"

I looked at my watch. I needed to hurry if I wanted to make it on time to the children's hospital.

"Nope," I answered, kissing him quickly on the cheek. "Tell them it's Smiley...Smiley the Clown."

it all starts with God

MICK THURBER

For of Him, and through Him, and to Him,

are all things: to whom be glory for ever.

ROMANS 11:36

C'mon. Think, Think! With my face buried in my hands, I must have muttered this to myself a hundred times, racking my brain in a desperate attempt to come up with the "big idea" for my advertising/graphic design class project. I was staring face to face at a major brain freeze, and time was running out fast. I had a great deal riding on this project—it was the first assignment of the most important course I had ever taken in college. I was starting my senior year, and I desperately needed to get on track with my major and turn some things around. I needed a good grade. Actually, I needed an outstanding grade. It was *essential* that I nailed a great concept, and I was down to just two days remaining to come up with a solution.

The assignment was to develop a cover layout for a new magazine called *America.* We were to design a logo identity for the title along with a strong visual concept and theme for the cover.

Working on a magazine cover was an exciting challenge, but it was quickly tempered with the reality of a short, "no-excuses" deadline and an outside, top-level design guru being brought in to scrutinize and critique our work.

A thousand ideas were spinning around in my mind, but nothing seemed to work. The clock was ticking-ticking-ticking, and the pressure was mounting. One thing was clear—I needed help. I started to pray.

I had been a Christian for three years and had grown accustomed to asking God for help. I knew He heard my prayers for the big, more important things, like praying for missionaries in foreign countries, blessing our country, or asking God to save my friends who had not yet come to know Him. But when I came to realize how deeply He cared for the "everyday" things in my life, like school…it blew me away.

So, with two days to go and nothing to show for my efforts but a blank pad of paper, I asked God to help me. I pleaded, *God, I need you right now. Help me to see the idea You have for me on this project. You know how important it is. You know how little time I have. Please give me the solution I need for my presentation. Thank you for your answers.*

It wasn't long at all before I began to feel the weight of my worries over this project, lifting. Just knowing that God was there to help brought a new sense of energy. New, solid ideas for the project started to materialize. I could feel the momentum building. At last, the *America* cover concept I had been searching for finally came to me. I quickly started sketching it out, and everything fell into place. The title design was strong. The concept was sound. I was thrilled! God came through again…in perfect timing.

After the layout was completed, the next step was to create the image used on the magazine cover. I was not an accomplished illustrator—more like an "illustrator-in-training." Once again I prayed, this time asking God to help me execute the idea He had already given me. I asked Him to help me capture the drama and emotion in the painting I envisioned…to give me a higher level of skill in creating the composition…to work through me, empowering me to get this done.

I was pumped! I was painting with all my heart. And I had a realization that I was painting for God. It felt incredible. I was amazed at the way it all came together. When the painting was finished I felt deeply grateful for God's answer to my prayer. I sensed the beginning of a new dimension in my life as I approached my work, a new purpose and plan.

I had asked God for help when I had nothing. He gave me the idea and then gave me the ability to work through and complete the concept. I, in turn, wanted to give God the glory for all He had taught me during the process.

When I presented my cover concept to the instructor, he quietly examined the layout for some time before discussing the direction I had taken. He said he was impressed with the concept and execution of my design. The instructor commented that this piece was a breakthrough for me and represented the level of work I had always been capable of doing. God had touched my life, and I found a new level of confidence in Him that day. I would never forget it.

I began to ask God for His help and guidance with all my classes. And then with everything I did! This idea of asking God for direction, totally depending on Him for the ability to do what He wanted of me, and then giving Him the glory was becoming an integral part of my life. His faithfulness was amazing.

One day at the university, during a library visit between classes, I felt impressed to read my Bible. I searched the second floor for an unoccupied cubicle. At last, I found one and began to read.

You know, sometimes God will surprise you with a life-changing moment when you least expect it. This day at the library was one of those times, a day that I would remember forever.

I was reading in the book of Romans, chapter 11, when I came upon a verse that was unfamiliar to me, verse 36. "For of Him, and through Him, and to Him, are all things: to whom be glory for ever." I read it again. "For of Him, and through Him, and to Him, are all things:" And again. And again!

All at once I realized this was huge. I knew in my heart, at that very moment, that this was God's plan for me on how to begin each new day, each new "assignment" that was put before me.

It was the same process, the same prayer that God had impressed on my heart during the magazine cover project and for the days that followed.

"For of Him" *God, give me the ideas and wisdom that I need for today.* "Through Him" *God, give me the power and ability to carry out the ideas and plans that you have me—even the ones that seem impossible.* "To Him" *I had acknowledged God and praised Him for helping me. The glory belonged to Him.*

Romans 11:36 changed my life forever and for good. It stuck. I've now been in the graphic design business for a number of years. With a possible exception or two, I have started each day of work with this verse. It has become my daily prayer, my source of confidence, and my devotion.

the diploma

MICHAEL T. POWERS

Then at last everyone will say,
"There truly is a reward for those who live for God;
surely there is a God who judges justly here on earth."

PSALM 58:11 NLT

"THROUGH PERSEVERANCE MANY PEOPLE WIN SUCCESS OUT OF WHAT SEEMED DESTINED TO BE CERTAIN FAILURE."

—Benjamin Disraeli

I was exhausted from working my two jobs over the weekend and was not looking forward to the graduation ceremony. I have been to many graduations, and I know how boring they are for most people. To top everything off, my wife and I had our two kids under the age of three with us. Both of the kids were squirming and whining, and I knew it was going to be a long afternoon. Our sole comic relief came when my three-year-old patted and rubbed the head of a bald man we did not know in front of us. As the ceremony dragged on, I kept thinking of all the places I would rather be and made up my mind that I wasn't going to enjoy myself.

It was your ordinary graduation ceremony: a hot, sweaty auditorium filled with people fanning themselves with their programs, listening to speech upon boring speech, and the endless calling of names as each matriculate walked across the stage to grab this piece of paper that symbolized his or her academic accomplishment. It was getting harder and harder to pay attention. Just as my attitude started to go sour, they began calling out the graduate's names. The classmates formed a single file line and made their way up towards the podium.

That's when I caught my first close-up glimpse of Kim. She looked up at us and was trying in vain to hold back the tears. She was not doing a good job of it. Believe me; holding back emotions is not something that Kim does very well. There she was, standing in line, about to receive her diploma, and she was probably thinking about a number of things. Maybe her dad who passed away a few years ago and didn't get to see her reach her goal, or her grandmother, who also passed away recently and who had always wanted to attend college, but her family didn't have the money…

For me it was like something from a movie. You know, the dramatic slow motion scene where all the crowd noise grows quiet, and the camera slowly moves up on her face as the tears begin to fall. She was a good distance away from us, but to me it was as if she were standing in front of me. That simple act of looking up at those loved ones who had come to watch her graduate, and gently rubbing the tears of joy, accomplishment, and pride out of her eyes really got through to me. The selfishness in me melted away, and I realized why I was there and not somewhere else.

"KIMBERLY ANNE CONWAY, GRADUATING MAGNA CUM LAUDE," came booming over the auditorium's sound system, and she walked gracefully across the huge stage and received this piece of paper that symbolized so many things to her. Then just before she walked off the stage, she turned around toward those who had come to share the day with her, and, with the brightest smile on her face, waved and grinned at us like a little girl getting on the school bus for the first time.

I glanced at my wife and saw the teardrops roll gently down as the love she had for her sister manifested itself on her face.

You see, Kim is not your ordinary college graduate. She is thirty-eight years old and has stuck with her goal of graduating from college for the past twenty years. It's not like she is going to look back on that part of her life, sigh, and say, "College...the best twenty years of my life!"

She attended college while working full time, and she studied extremely hard, especially the past couple of years as she pushed toward her goal of a college degree. Many times she felt like quitting, and, if it weren't for her support group of other nontraditional students that cared for her, she would have given up on her goal. Many times she would call one of the other students she knew and tell them she wanted to quit, and would be talked out of it. Then a while later this student would call her and say she wanted to quit, and Kim would talk her out of it... (Luckily, they both didn't want to quit at the same time!)

I have the utmost respect for Kim. It takes a special person to stick with a goal as long as she has. I attended college for three years when I got out of high school, but I stopped when I wasn't sure what I wanted to do with my life. Many times I have looked back and wished that I had stuck with it and gone on to be a high school teacher. If for no other reason, I wish I had finished something that I had started.

I know what it feels like to walk out of that last final exam of the semester, breathe in the fresh air just outside the doors of the university, and feel like the weight of the world has been lifted off your shoulders for at least a little while. I can't even begin to imagine what it felt like for Kim after so many years...

I love you, Kim, and I want you to know that I admire you for that symbolic piece of paper that will soon adorn a wall in your house.

In the words of Caleb, my three-year-old: "HAPPY GRADULATION, AUNT KIMMY!"

mr. hope!

DARLA SATTERFIELD DAVIS

There is surely a future hope for you,

and your hope will not be cut off.

PROVERBS 23:18 NIV

"I'm sorry," the Financial Aide Officer said. "I just don't see how you could possibly make it here. You have no money, no one to help you, and you are a single mother with a young child. I wish I could help, but I would hate to see you start and not be able to finish," she said shaking her head. I thanked her for her honesty, left the college, and drove home despondent.

A year passed, and I was back at the same Christian college on the same "College Days" event; but this time I knew what my friend was reaching for was out of range for me. I began to laugh and talk in the long lines with my friend as we went from place to place, and continued with my unsolicited but humorous views on college and life in general. To my embarrassment, a man in a suit came up to me and asked if he could have a word with me. I thought I might be in trouble for my antics and was all set to apologize.

"Please step in my office" he said. "Have a seat won't you? I sat down nervously. "Listen," he began, "I have been watching you all day, and I like your spunk and attitude." He said without changing expressions. "I understand that you applied here last year, but were advised against coming."

"Yes, Sir," I answered sheepishly, "I really can't afford this college, and I am still a single mother, so nothing has really changed. I am just here to support a friend."

"Well, let me tell you something young lady," he said leaning forward in his chair. If you want to come here badly enough, you can make it." He narrowed his eyes and looked more intently at me. "It will be the hardest thing you have ever done in your life, but if you really want it, you can make it happen," he said. I looked solemnly at him for a few minutes and weighed his words carefully. "Has anyone else in my situation ever made it?" I asked still staring at him. "Not many I can tell you, probably less than I can count on two hands for sure." He returned. I paused for a few seconds, "Well, that's all I needed to know sir. Sign me up; I will be here this fall." As I shook hands with the man, I glanced down at the nameplate on his desk. "Mr. Dave Hope" it read; I had to smile at the irony.

Four years later, when I walked across the stage, got my diploma, and shook hands with the faculty and staff, I gripped Mr. Hope's hand and thanked him. "You didn't lie, Mr. Hope, you sure didn't lie. This has been so hard, but I guess I did want it bad enough after all. Thank You. Thank you for giving me...Hope!"

the day the cheering stopped

JOHN C. STEWART

(as told to Gloria Cassity Stargel; names in this story have been changed)

"There is rejoicing in the presence of the angels

of God over one sinner who repents."

LUKE 15:10 NIV

It happened on a cold day in January, midway through my senior year in high school. I tossed my books into the locker and reached for my black-and-gold Cougar jacket. From down the corridor, a friend called out, "Good luck, Johnny. I hope you get the school you want!"

Playing football was more than a game to me. It was my *life*. So the world looked pretty wonderful as I headed up the hill toward the gym to learn which college wanted me on their team.

How I counted on the this scholarship—I had for years! It held my only hope for higher education. My dad, an alcoholic, had left home long ago, and Mom worked two jobs just to keep seven children fed. I even held down part-time jobs to help out.

But I wasn't worried. I had the grades I needed. And ever since grammar school, I had lived and breathed football. It was my entire identity.

Growing up in a little southern town where football is king, my skills on the field made me a big man in the community as well as on my high-school campus. I pictured myself right up there on a pedestal—where most people would place me.

Everyone helped to pump up my ego. The local newspaper mentioned me in write-ups; at football games exuberant cheerleaders yelled out my name; people constantly made comments like, "You can do it, Johnny. You can go all the way to professional football!" And I ate it up. In a way, it made up for my not having a dad to encourage me along the way.

Hurrying to the gym that day, I recalled all those football games—and all those *injuries!* I never had let any of them slow me down for long—not the broken back or the messed up shoulders and knees—I just gritted my teeth and played right through the agony. I *had* to.

And now came the reward. A good future would be worth the price I had paid. So with a confident grin on my face, I sauntered into Coach Stone's office.

Coach sat behind his desk, the papers from my file spread before him. Our three other coaches sat around the room. No doubt about it, this lineup signaled a momentous occasion.

"Have a seat, Johnny," Coach motioned to the chair beside his desk. "Johnny," he started, "you've worked really hard. You've done a good job for us. A couple of colleges want to make you an offer." Something about his tone made me nervous. I shifted my sitting position.

"But, Johnny," he said, holding my medical records in his hands, "Doctor Kendley can't recommend you for college football. Johnny, one more bad hit, and you could be paralyzed for life. We can't risk it."

A long silence followed. Then Coach Stone's eyes met mine. "I'm sorry, Johnny. There will be no scholarship."

No scholarship? The blow hit me like a 300-pound linebacker slamming against my chest. Somehow I got out of that office. I could not seem to understand that they were thinking of my welfare. Instead, all I could think was, *You're not good enough, you're not good enough, you're not good enough.*

For *me,* the cheering stopped. Without the cheering, I was nothing. And without college, I would *stay* a nothing.

After that, I just gave up. And in so doing, I lost my grip on life.

At first, I settled for beer and marijuana. Soon I got into the hard stuff: acid, PCP, heroin, cocaine—I tried them all. By the time graduation rolled around, I wonder how I even made it through the ceremonies.

Several older friends tried to talk to me about God. Yet even though I had grown up in church, had even served as an altar boy, I couldn't grasp the fact that God had anything to do with my present situation.

A couple of buddies and I decided to hit the road. We had no money and no goal. Along the way, we got into stealing gas to keep us going. When we got hungry enough, we picked up some odd jobs. No matter how little food we had, we always managed to get more drugs.

My anger continued to build. It wasn't long until I got into a bad fight and landed in jail thousands of miles from home. It caused me to take a good look at myself and see how low I had sunk. *God,* I prayed for the first time in years, *please help me. I'm lost, and I can't find my way back.*

I didn't hear an immediate answer. Nor did I clean up my act. We *did* head toward home, but the old car had had enough. It quit.

I went into a garage, hoping to get some cheap parts. *Maybe I can patch her up enough to get us home.* I was tired, hungry, dirty—and very much under the influence. Yet a man there extended a hand of friendship. He even took us to supper. After we were fed, Mr. Brown called me aside, "Son," he said, "you don't have to live like this. You can be somebody if only you'll try. God will help you. Remember, He loves you. And so do I."

I was buffaloed. He seemed to care about me. And he had called me "son." It had been a long, long time since a man had called me "son."

That night, in my sleeping bag, I gazed up at the star-filled Texas night. The sky looked so close, I thought maybe I could reach up and touch it. And once again, I tried to pray. *Lord, I am so tired. If You'll have me, I'm ready to come back to You.*

In my heart, I heard God answer, *I'm here. Come on back, son. I'm here.* He called me "son," just like Mr. Brown did. I liked that.

On the road again, I got to thinking: *If Mr. Brown, a complete stranger, thinks I can make something of myself, maybe I can.*

I didn't straighten out all at once. But at least I started trying. And God kept sending people to help me. Like Susan. In

September, this cute young thing—a casual friend from high school—came up to me at a football game, of all places. She kissed me on the cheek, and said, "Welcome home, Johnny."

The day she said, "Johnny, if you keep doing drugs, I can't date you anymore," was the day I quit them for good.

Susan and I married, and today we have three beautiful children. We're active in our local church and operate a successful business. I can tell you it means the world to me to have earned the respect of my community.

All these years later, I still can feel the sting of that day—the day the cheering stopped. The hurt doesn't linger though, as I've learned I can live without the cheers of a human crowd. After all, I have a caring Heavenly Father who calls me "son." And I do have a cheering section—a Heavenly one. Check out this Bible verse I discovered: "There is rejoicing in the presence of the angels of God over one sinner who repents" (Luke 15:10 NIV).

How about that?

Angels! Cheering for *ME!*

I like that.

if you're gonna quit, don't tell daddy!

MAX DAVIS

If anybody does sin, we have one who speaks to the Father in our defense—Jesus Christ, the Righteous One.

1 JOHN 2:1 NIV

I'm almost certain that the day I popped into this world, my dad was standing right there in the delivery room with a football in his hands, anxiously waiting.

From the moment I was born, it was my dad's dream that his boy play football. He grew up milking cows at 3:30 every morning and again at 4:30 every afternoon and never got the chance to play, though he wanted to terribly. So, I guess the next best thing was a son he could live his dream through.

As a result, I played seventeen years of football—from the third grade all the way through college and then had an appalling tryout in the old USFL. It must be said here, however, that my dad never forced me. He let it be known, early on, that it was my decision to play, not his. But you know, I really wanted to please him, and that made me work just a little bit harder—a lot harder.

When most kids were flipping burgers at McDonalds or serving up snow cones, I was running stadiums and pumping iron. In the summers, I did work for my Dad's air conditioning business, but he made sure I went home early every afternoon to work out for football. My senior year of high school, Dad told me he'd give me $100 for every touchdown I scored. His motivation must have worked because I scored twenty-two that year, setting a school record, and racking up $2,200 in the process!

And did I mention that my Dad was at every single game I ever played and almost every practice? I came to depend on him being present. When warming up before a game my stomach would be in knots until I'd spot my Dad in the stands. As soon as I saw him, a calm would wash over me, and I was ready to play. I guess all the hard work, motivation, and support paid off, because I was fortunate enough to get a full-ride athletic scholarship to the University of Mississippi.

Oh, had I made my dad proud! And have mercy on your soul if you happened to run into him at the coffee shop or the café! Every word out of his mouth was, "My boy" this and "My boy" that. Yes, sir, I had made my dad some kind of proud. So, you can imagine what happened on the day that I did the unthinkable...I quit the team.

I wasn't getting the playing time that I thought I deserved, and I wasn't happy. Plus, I was having a rough time in general. One morning at about 4 A.M., I packed my bags, snuck out of the dorm, and quit—throwing away my complete athletic scholarship and along with it all those years of hard work and dreams.

My home was six hours South, and because I knew how disappointed and angry Dad was going to be, I did the only sensible thing I knew to do—I drove in the opposite direction—North!

I drove due North on Interstate 155 for over six hours until I was almost in St. Louis, Missouri. Terrified, with tears blurring my vision, I had a lump in the pit of my stomach—that uneasy feeling you get when you know you have made a big mistake. The entire drive I was beating myself up thinking, *What are you going to do with your life? You've just thrown away your scholarship. You stupid idiot! You've really blown it big time!* Now the tears flowed like rivers down my cheeks.

Finally, at some point near the outskirts of St. Louis, I realized there was really only one thing to do. I had to go home and face my fears—mainly, Dad. I whipped my 1979 Monte Carlo around and drove twelve hours south to Baton Rouge, Louisiana.

Worn out and ragged from my emotional turmoil, not to mention an eighteen-hour drive, I at last turned onto Leadale Drive. It was about 10:00 P.M. and from the street, I could see the light on in the living room and knew that Mama and Dad were sitting there watching TV.

Scared senseless, I just drove around the block for I don't know how long, until I mustered up enough courage to go knock on the door. When I did, and Mama answered, I burst into the house, crying—not because I quit football, not because I was going to miss it, not because I had thrown away a full scholarship—but because I knew how much I had let my dad down.

I sat there in the middle of the living room floor repeating over and over again, "I quit the team! I quit the team! I'm such an idiot! I can't believe I actually quit!"

For the longest time, Dad didn't say a word. He just sat in his Lazy-Boy and rocked quietly, pondering the situation. Finally, Mama broke the silence. "Jimmy!" she said. "Do something! Can't you see your son is in trouble?" I always was "his" son when I messed up.

Me, I was fully expecting to get railed on—for Dad to yell and carry on—say something to the tune of, "Yes, you are an idiot! You really blew it! I can't believe you would do such and such. After all our years of hard work, you just flushed it down the toilet!"

But Dad didn't do anything of the sort. Instead, he looked up from his chair and in a soft tone of compassion said, "Son, there's only one thing we can do."

I wiped a tear from my face and asked, "What's that?"

"We have to go tomorrow and ask Coach Sloan to take you back."

"I can't go back!" I protested. "They'll never take me. Plus they'll laugh me back off campus!"

"Son, I know it's going to be hard, but this is something we have to do," he said, "And I'll go with you. Now, go take a shower and get some rest, then in the morning we will go."

I tossed and turned in bed that night, yet, I had a strange peace that came with the unexpected and compassionate support of my Dad. When morning arrived, Mama had cooked a killer breakfast. My Dad and I ate homemade biscuits and gravy with bacon and eggs and then got in my car and drove six hours North to Oxford, Mississippi.

You know, during that whole drive, Dad never once put me down or belittled me, and as far as I could tell he didn't act disappointed in me. Instead of a six-hour lecture, that drive became one of the most powerful bonding times between my dad and me.

When we finally made it to the coach's office, Dad looked up at me and said, "Okay, Son, this is something you have to do. I can't go in for you."

I was shaking pretty hard, but Dad rubbed my shoulder, calming me and giving me courage. I went in, faced the coach, and, remarkably, he took me back. My dad took a bus home that day. What a dad!

I went on to finish my four years on full scholarship and graduated with a degree in Journalism. It wasn't until more than twenty-something years later, looking back, that I saw with clarity what an incredible act of wisdom and love that was. That very experience helped me to grasp God's grace.

When we mess up, and we do, our natural tendency is to run in the opposite direction from God. We think that God is disappointed in us and that we must clean up our act before we go to Him. So we hide because we are scared and positive that God is not interested in us. We're absolutely sure He is going to rail on us.

We feel this way because so often we do get railed upon, not by God, but by super-zealots and pious-pumpkins who have little or no understanding of grace. Yet, God calls out to us almost pleading, *Come on, Son. Come on, Daughter. I know you blew it. I know you messed up. But it doesn't matter. Come on anyway. Get in the car with Me. I want to go with you. I want to support you and help you overcome what you're going through. I'll give you strength to do what you have to do. Do you hear me condemning you? No. Now come on. This is going to be a bonding time for us. You'll know Me so much better after this. But you have to trust Me.*

If my dad would have condemned and belittled me, chances are I would not have gone back and finished my education. Criticism and belittling bind us, grace frees us.

That day changed my life forever as I learned the power of God-inspired grace.

his ways are not ours

CANDY ARRINGTON

"For my thoughts are not your thoughts,

neither are your ways my ways," declares the LORD.

ISAIAH 55:8 NIV

Sitting across the desk from my high school headmaster, I could see his mouth moving, but was having trouble processing his words. Forcing myself to focus, I heard him say, "I'm sorry to have to tell you this, but the school is closing. We've lost necessary financial backing. This is difficult for all of us."

Difficult? I was shattered! In a matter of minutes, my carefully constructed plans vanished. My senior year tilted, slid, and crashed like an upended banquet table laden with a feast. I was left to sift through the resulting mess.

Plastering a polished-veneer-of-a-face across my chaotic thoughts, I traced my steps back through the halls of the old mansion that had been my academic home for the past four years. Once outside, the sweltering August heat enveloped me. I sat in my steamy car, shocked, trying to make sense of what I'd just heard.

My last year of high school was going to be a breeze. With only senior English necessary for graduation, I looked forward to a light course load of fun electives, a couple of hours a week working in the school office, a job as yearbook editor, and a shortened schedule with early dismissal. It was going to be a great year. Then came the announcement that the school was closing. I was faced with an enormous decision. Should I complete my high school education at the public high school or move to another private school in town? In either case, it would be a difficult adjustment as I tried to fit in and make new friends.

I retreated to my room for several days to ponder the options and pray. For the most part, I adopted a woe-is-me attitude and couldn't understand why God would allow this to happen. After all, I had everything planned. Despite my own efforts at trying to resolve the situation, I finally reached a moment of revelation when I realized the decision really wasn't up to me. I read the words of Jeremiah 29:11-13 (NIV), "For I know the plans I have for you" declares the LORD, "plans to prosper you and not to harm you, plans to give you hope and a future....Call upon me and come and pray to me, and I will listen to you. You will seek me and find me when you seek me with all your heart." The discovery of this verse and much prayer prepared me for the impossible option that soon presented itself.

"Let's go over to Wofford College and see about getting you enrolled," my father calmly stated.

"Daddy, I can't go to college because I haven't even graduated from high school yet!" I replied.

His suggestion seemed preposterous for a number of reasons. In addition to my status as a non-graduate, the college had only recently gone co-ed. Only a few girls had been admitted and none of them with the handicap of not being a high school graduate. Also, I had yet to take the SAT. In my mind, I was definitely not yet college material. But my father persisted.

As we sat in the Dean of Admissions office, the situation seemed anything but hopeful.

"I'd be willing to wager you've been pampered at that private school. There won't be anyone here to walk you through your assignments or hold your hand. This is college!" blustered the Dean.

I nodded and managed to squeak out, "I know. But I think I can handle it."

Perhaps he caught a hint of my determination in my words because he paused and slowly smiled. More than likely, it was God softening his heart and paving the way for my journey down an unexpected path.

"Very well," came the Dean's thundering voice. "I'll let you give it a try. I accept you as a probationary freshman. We'll see what you can do."

The fact that I had no high school diploma was never mentioned, and the next week I registered for classes. Upon completing my first semester, I discovered that I had made the Dean's list. Because of the college prep courses I'd taken in high school, my classes were not as academically challenging as the Dean implied they would be. I made friends quickly, enjoyed my studies, and was happy.

Following my freshman year, I received a note from the Dean stating, "I'm delighted to say, you proved me wrong. Congratulations!"

The journey to college without graduating from high school was the first of many unexpected twists on the path of my life. At the time, I didn't realize that my decision to major in English in college would one day result in a writing career. However, I've learned that if I allow God to lead the way and direct my steps, He can take unlikely and improbable situations and turn them into something beneficial, because with God nothing is impossible.

In the eyes of the world, the chances of a high school undergraduate being admitted to college and graduating with honors were remote. To God, it was only a tiny blip in His ultimate plan for my life. God's ways of accomplishing that plan are beyond my ability to understand. And without a doubt, I'm thankful He is in control.

a certain smile

DARLA SATTERFIELD DAVIS

**"The only thing that counts is faith
expressing itself through love."**

GALATIANS 5:6 NIV

I had been crying for more than an hour when a friend called.
I gasped a few words into the phone. "I'm alright…gasp…I am
just so tired…gasp…I am overwhelmed and I just can't think…
gasp, gasp…I will be fine…really…I just need to get some sleep
and try to think what to do" I choked. My college buddy was
nearly 10 years younger than I, and male. He couldn't possibly
understand what going to school, raising a child alone, and
trying to work all at the same time meant.

I have never been worth much when I let myself get beyond
the point of exhaustion, and I was more than tired that night.
There were baskets of laundry in the living room and dishes in
the sink. The dryer was buzzing, my daughter was sobbing in her

room after I told her I couldn't help with a science project because my term paper was due at 7:30 in the morning, and she had just spilled milk all over my notes! The landlord had called wanting to be paid, and once again the child support for that month had not come; and to top it all off, I had a flat tire. I was a sophomore in college; too far in to drop out, too far from the finish line to imagine ever crossing it.

Twenty minutes later the Vice President of the college and two professors were at my door. I was shocked and horrified at the same time. "May we come in?" asked the Vice President. "Oh, I...oh, it is such a mess in here, I...did Jeff call you?...I am so sorry!...I told him I am fine...I am...really...I am *SO embarrassed...*" I stammered, wishing I could melt into the floor and knowing I must have looked like a gargoyle from crying so hard.

"We didn't come to see your house; we came to see you" Dr. Wright said and gently put his hand on my shoulder. We know how hard this is for you. We just wanted to stop by and encourage you, and see if we could help in any way." He said kindly. "Oh no! I am...I am just really overtired...I am just a little overwhelmed, but I will be fine tomorrow...really, he shouldn't have called you!" I stammered and fell over my words.

"Darla is in my Entrepreneur Class," Dr. Wright nodded to his companions to follow him inside. "I have to tell you, how impressed I am with your comments and participation, Darla. You really add to the class, and give such insightful perspectives." Dr. Wright said with sincerity. I was surprised he even took notice I was in his class; I wasn't even a business major. "Darla, You *are* going to be fine. You *are* going to make it!" He continued. "I know you are tired, but I know you have what it takes to pull this off!" He said not letting me drop my gaze.

"When you graduate, do you know who hands you your diploma?...I do", he said smiling. "I am going to be there the day you graduate, and I am going to look right at you when I call your name, and smile. At that moment, you and I will remember this day when you wanted to give it all up...but didn't," he said with such surety that I couldn't help but believe him.

I did survive that night, finished my term paper, helped with the science project, and did the laundry and dishes. Some friends even stopped by and "happened to have" a tire for my car with them!

Two years later, Dr. Hal Wright called out my name, and good to his word, he turned, we smiled *that smile,* and he handed me my diploma. I will never forget that man, or the fact that he had faith in me even when I couldn't believe in myself. Faith is an amazing tool. It is the ability to see beyond our circumstances and into the possibilities—that flicker of hope that turns everything around.

the graduate

AMANDA PILGRIM

Let us not become weary in doing [well], for at the proper time we will reap a harvest if we do not give up.

GALATIANS 6:9 NIV

I searched the stage until I found her smiling face. There she sat in the middle of her class, in a black robe with her tassel swinging to and fro, face beaming. The gymnasium was full of excited family members and friends, all here to support their young graduates. My reason for being here was very different. I didn't have a child or just a friend walking across the stage to accept a diploma that day. I was there for my mother.

The odds had been stacked against her from the beginning. The university itself had told her it would be nearly impossible for a single mother, with no outside financial help, to successfully attain a degree. Family members although hopeful, always kept a hesitant attitude about her ability to complete the immense task before her. But she did it. I still marvel at her determination.

She spent many tearful hours asking God to give her strength to see her goal to the end. I remember watching her as she would shut a book with frustration and cry that she couldn't do it anymore, only to pick it up later and begin to study twice as hard. I remember standing at the window watching as she left for work at five o'clock in the morning so she could be back in time to take classes that afternoon and evening. But, what I remember most is the look on her face as she put that robe on and prepared to walk down the aisle and make her dream a reality.

My mother earned her teaching degree that warm day in May, but she taught me many, very valuable lessons long before she was "licensed" to teach. She taught me that it takes courage to stand up for what you believe and to accomplish your dreams in the face of adversity and opposition. She taught me that you are never too old to have a dream and take the steps to see them become a reality. Most importantly, she taught me that with God all things are truly possible.

I thank God every night for giving me such a wonderful mother and mentor. Through her struggles and eventual successes, I learned what it really means to trust and live out God's plan for my life.

a heart that lasts forever

JOAN CLAYTON

Now these three remain: faith, hope and love.

But the greatest of these is love

1 CORINTHIANS 13:13 NIV

I believe every child in my room was there not by accident, but placed by God. Each one became my forever friend, and I formed a love in my heart that I could never let go. Such was Robert.

He came to my second grade classroom with his older married sister as an interpreter. He found his nametag and seated himself while placing his supplies just so on his desk.

Those big black eyes told me volumes about him, and his broad smile welcomed me into his young life. He was small in stature but had a big heart; I knew God had sent me another gift.

Robert was the youngest child in a close-knit family. They might not have had much in material possessions, but they were millionaires in love. I relished the interest his older sister took in Robert's accomplishments shown by her frequent visits. His family came to our school many times to admire his work, to smile at me and shake my hand, and always presented me with a goodbye hug. They seemed to appreciate my efforts to dialog with them in broken Spanish.

At the end of the first day of school, I found my first "I love you" note from Robert. Before the school year ended, I had 180 notes from him, a love note for each day. I still have them today.

Robert's superior work and creativity, especially in art, told me volumes about his future. I relished each day, knowing in my heart I was one day closer to my retirement. Looking back, it was my greatest year. I simply loved the children more than ever, and they seemed to learn more than ever.

Before I knew it, the school year had ended. "This is for you Mrs. Clayton. I will miss you. I love you." Holding back my tears was not an option. Robert handed me a used Barbie doll with a make-do dress of red and yellow crepe paper that stood in a glass vase. Red ribbons around the vase held two tiny hearts tied with love by little chubby hands. One heart read "Robert," the other "Mrs. Clayton." I wondered if Robert had to sacrifice something he loved to give me this gift. Did he have to trade something he treasured with one of his siblings?

His family also came to tell me goodbye. Robert's dad hugged me and handed me an envelope. Inside was a one-dollar bill with a note: "Un regalo para ti con muchas gracias para enseñar nos hijito." (A present for you with many thanks for teaching our little son.) This time the tears burst into a river. With a widow's mite and a heart of love I had received the gift of all gifts. I still have the dollar and will keep it always.

Robert's parents had supported me all year. We had become close friends as we laughed at my Spanish with a southern accent. I looked forward to seeing them at parent conferences, parties, and other activities but now the time I had to share in Robert's life would be given to the third grade teacher. Robert left me with a piece of his heart.

The next year I received many phone calls from Robert. "Mrs. Clayton, this is Robert. I just wanted to tell you. I...uh...well, I...uh, I just want to say Mrs. Clayton, I just want to say, well....I just want to say 'I love you.'"

As a third grader Robert called and invited me to an art show where his work had won first prize. I beamed with pride as he led me around showing me his creations.

In sixth grade, Robert invited me to his graduating class that would be entering junior high. He made a beautiful speech. He immediately came down the steps to hug his family and me. I cried.

Robert's phone calls were not as frequent after that, and I understood completely. He was growing up, and I thrilled upon reading about his many accomplishments in our local newspaper.

One day in late May I received a phone call. "Mrs. Clayton, I love you." I recognized the voice immediately. "This is Robert. Remember me? I was in your class the year you retired."

"Well, thank you Robert. After ten years you still remember me?"

"I could never forget you, Mrs. Clayton. I'm calling to see if you could come to my high school graduation. It's Saturday afternoon at 1 o'clock."

"My husband and I will be there, and thank you so much!"

We left early since we had to drive a distance to his high school. I told Emmitt about all the wonderful things I remembered about Robert and his family. He could hardly wait to meet them.

We found a seat and began to read our program. Imagine my excitement when I saw Robert's name as "Valedictorian." Of course that didn't come as a surprise. I had always known his potential.

Robert gave a marvelous valedictory address. He spoke of wonderful heights to be achieved, persistence in seeking the good, and having the determination to never give up. My pride in him could not be measured. He then gave his speech in beautiful Spanish. I loved every minute of it!

After that I heard Robert saying, "Now I want to honor a person who has had a profound affect upon my life. She set me on a path in second grade that led me to success." He reached under the podium and pulled out a big cuddly brown teddy bear. "Mrs. Clayton, this is for you."

I lost it! I mean, lost it! Tears dropped from everyone.

Robert walked down the steps and walked toward me in the audience, holding out the teddy bear to me. I literally ran to meet him, crying all the way. He cried too, and we hugged a long time while the audience clapped.

After the ceremony, Robert's dad walked up with a bouquet of yellow carnations and several cards written in Spanish. With tears in his eyes he hugged me and kept repeating, "Gracias hermosa maestra!" While I couldn't keep up with all the Spanish, his body language and his eyes spoke volumes of love.

At home I opened my beautiful cards. I read them ever so slowly and savored every word. Translated, they read: "In the most painful fights of life, when so much crookedness is around us and we cry, there is one love who will always love you, and one that will never forget you."

Signed by Robert's Dad

"You showed me how to read, you showed me how to sing, you showed me how to succeed. In this day I dedicate and send one kiss from a loveable child who loves you."

Signed by Robert's Mom

"Dear Mrs. Clayton, thank you for always supporting me and giving me faith in myself. I will always cherish everything you've shown me and I'll make sure I pass on all your knowledge. Thank you so much and I know God will keep blessing you for everything you've done."

I love you, Robert

The Barbie doll still stands atop my desk that contains the files that are stuffed with love notes from children I have taught. Every May I relive my last days of school memories and wish I could start all over again.

I have to be the happiest ex-teacher in the world. Thirty-one years of teaching children gave me a child's heart, and that is a heart that lasts forever!

"And now these three remain: faith, hope and love. But the greatest of these is love." 1 Corinthians 13:13 (NIV)

she's earned it

MICHAEL T. POWERS

Those who came before us will teach you.

They will teach you from the wisdom of former generations.

JOB 8:10 NLT

Teachers do a thankless job for an obscenely low pay check, and many times there are no short term "rewards" as they are often left wondering if they are getting through to their students.

I would encourage you to make an attempt to write to those men and women who have touched your life through their gift of teaching. The simple act of a card or letter, even if you haven't seen them in twenty years, will allow them to realize that they have made a difference in the lives of their students. And hey, if you are currently a student, I'm sure it would be good for your high school or college career to let your present teachers know they are doing a good job! (That and a nice, big, shiny, red apple!)

Dear Senator Kohl,

I have had the privilege of knowing Karen Mullen, first as a teacher, and now as someone I have chosen to edit my first book. There is no one who prepared me more for college than did Mrs. Mullen. She encouraged my love of reading and writing, helped develop a love for classic literature through her choice of authors to study, and gave me some life lessons that I will never forget.

We did not just read a textbook, do homework on it, and get tested on the material in her classes. We were allowed to have open discussion after each story, sometimes veering away from the subject matter at hand, but always pertaining to something that we as students were interested in. She was tough but fair and earned the respect if not the love of all her students.

Most classes in high school I breezed through with a minimal amount of work. I rarely had any school work that I took home. Not that our teachers didn't push us, it was just that I was able to figure out most of what was going on and finish assignments while the teacher was still talking about them. That was until I had Mrs. Mullen. I was nudged, stretched, and sometimes jolted out of my academic cruise control by her. For the first time in my high school career, I was working on assignments at home, and most of those dealt with writing papers. We wrote papers, and then we wrote some more papers. I didn't appreciate her style of education until I got to college. After my first few weeks of university life, I was grateful for Mrs. Mullen. If it weren't for her classes in high school, college would have been a total shock for me.

Not only did she prepare me for college, she also changed my reading habits. Growing up, I had two genres that I read, and two only—epic fantasy, like *The Lord of the Rings,* and wildlife and outdoor fiction. When study hall came, I was usually caught up with my homework and would read for the entire period. During the first year I had her as a teacher in American Literature, I began to branch out and read the classics, but not just when we had an assignment. No, for the first time in my life I began to read Thoreau, Melville, and Poe for the pure pleasure of reading.

Toward the end of the first quarter of my senior year, my parents came to see Mrs. Mullen during one of the regularly scheduled parent/teacher conferences. I had straight A's that first quarter…or so I thought. There in front of Mrs. Mullen was a sheet of paper listing all the grades I was going to receive. Every teacher was giving me an A, except for Mrs. Mullen. She was giving me a B+ in her Psychological Literature class. Let me rephrase that. I was *earning* a B+ in her class. She told my folks that she felt bad that I wasn't going to get straight A's, but that I hadn't earned it. A B+, although close to an A, was still a B+.

My first thoughts were, *How much difference can there be between an A- and a B+? I was a good student, didn't get into trouble, and she couldn't give me an A, especially since straight A's would have been the result?* But the more I thought about it, the more I realized that I hadn't earned it, and that I would have to work harder the next quarter. That B+ stuck out like a sore thumb on my report card, but it was a motivating factor for me.

The following quarter, and the rest of my senior year, I earned straight A's. And the first one to come up and congratulate me was Mrs. Mullen after my second report card.

I leave you with a story I heard once that sums up my feelings toward my favorite high school teacher:

In ancient times a king decided to find and honor the greatest person among his subjects. A man of wealth and property was singled out. Another was praised for his healing powers; another for his wisdom and knowledge of the law. Still another was lauded for his business acumen. Many other successful people were brought back to the palace, and it became evident that the task of choosing the greatest would be difficult. Finally, the last candidate stood before the king. It was a woman. Her hair was white. Her eyes shown with the light of knowledge, understanding, and love.

"Who is this?" asked the king. "What has she done?"

"You have seen and heard all the others," said the king's aide. "This is their teacher."

The people applauded, and the king came down from his throne to honor her.

It is my hope that you also honor Karen Mullen. She's earned it.

Sincerely,

Michael T. Powers

Note from Michael: It is with great pleasure that I report that Mrs. Mullen did indeed win the coveted 2001 Kohl Foundation Teacher Award. Way to go Mrs. Mullen!

graduation in español

AMANDA PILGRIM

"I can do all things through Christ who strengthens me."

PHILIPPIANS 4:13 NKJV

He stood in my classroom visibly nervous. It was the first time we had met, and I must confess that I was a bit nervous myself. I kept thinking to myself, *How am I going to teach this young man his studies if he can't even speak English?*

I smiled at him and welcomed him to our class. We were already halfway through the year, and I didn't know how I was going to catch this student up to where he needed to be *and* teach him basic language skills. I prayed many times for God to give me the wisdom needed to help guide this student.

He was very polite and eager to learn which made things easier for the both of us. It was quite an interesting first week to say the least. The only verbal communication he gave was when he would step up to my desk and ask me, "Mr. Pilgrim, bathroom, yes?" It became quite an amusing challenge for everyone as we tried to remind him that I was a Mrs. not a Mr.

Juan would stay after school sometimes for an hour or more and ask questions in broken English about his work, and I in turn would try to answer in equally broken Spanish. I borrowed several workbooks from the teachers in the lower grades, and we began with the basics of the English language.

Juan studied extremely hard and completed every workbook I assigned to him. His American foster parents supported his academic achievement by encouraging him to speak English rather than Spanish at home. Juan began to blossom. He made friends quickly and became very popular as a soccer player. He worked diligently in the classroom and asked for books to read in order to help improve his English. He never tired of learning.

Working in a private Christian school, we had daily Bible classes, and they soon became Juan's favorite subject. He seemed to be captivated by the information we discussed in class concerning God and His will for our lives. He asked many questions about the Bible and was fascinated with the story of Salvation.

Juan never gave up and never quit trying when it came to his studies. He worked on his English by reading various books and practicing with the other students. He became a class project. His classmates would find new ways to help Juan understand and learn the English language.

Juan graduated from Jr. High that year in the top percentage of his class despite his language barrier. He gave a speech the day of his graduation about the hard work and dedication all of his classmates and family put forth to help him not only graduate and learn English but to also learn the meaning of God's love.

Juan will be graduating from High School this May. He never forgot his lessons on faith and working hard towards God's will for his life. He has traveled back to Mexico several times to visit his family and has used that time to teach them about Christ. He speaks English fluently and works in the church as an interpreter for Spanish speaking families and new members.

Through this experience I was reminded that success in life is not determined so much by what life presents to us in the way of obstacles and handicaps but rather by the attitude we choose when facing those challenges; it's not so much about what happens to us as it is about how much we trust God to see us through. What a shining example Juan is—of hope, purpose, and diligence.

from snob to servant

MURIEL LARSON

**"How can you think of saying, 'Let me
help you get rid of that speck in your eye,'
when you can't see past the log in your own eye?"**

MATTHEW 7:4 NLT

As a preacher's kid, I lived a somewhat sheltered life. When I saw a scroungy-looking geek, I cringed inside. *How repulsive!* I thought self-righteously. When I walked across the campus, I'd see this nerd sitting by himself. I never considered stopping to talk to him. What would people think of me talking to someone with thick glasses and greasy hair? God wouldn't ask me to do that!

After graduation, however, God gave me a job that would knock the Pharisee out of me and revolutionize my thinking and future. My father had talked to his good friend, Chief McCarthy, about the possibility of me working with him at the Middletown Police Department. One day Chief McCarthy called me and asked me to come down for an interview. The next day I started work at the Police Department.

EYE-OPENING JOB

I couldn't believe the people I had to work with! Many of them smelled as if they had climbed out of a sewer. The bleary eyes of those on drugs made them look like creatures from a sci-fi scene.

Then I met Art. He spoke to these kids so kindly—like they were people—human beings. "What's gone wrong in your life?" he'd ask. "How can we help you get on a better path? Let's talk about your problems."

One day as I looked in the eyes of a young woman, I realized she was hurting. I realized that in looking for something that would fulfill her life, she had chosen drugs. And suddenly I knew why I was there. I had something better to give these people.

DRUG RAID

One night I went on a drug raid with officers and other employees of the department. As we went in, an eerie feeling came over me, as if there were something evil about the place. It sent a chill down my back.

Psychedelic music blared through the dirty, messy house. It reeked with a strange odor. Kids under the influence of drugs were lying all over. We took thirty of them in. Most of their parents couldn't believe that their teenager was involved in drugs.

The girl I took into custody was from an upper-class home. Curious, I asked her, "What church do you go to?" She shrugged her shoulders and let me know that her family didn't go to church.

I could have been just like her, I thought. *If I didn't have Jesus in my life, who knows? Maybe I'd be trying to fill my life with drugs, the way she's doing.*

EX-PHARISEE SURRENDERS

That night I totally surrendered everything: my pride, my plans, even my relationships. And as for my pride, I faced up to the fact that we all are sinners, whether we're proud Pharisees, white liars, or dirty drug users. Christ died for us all!

My new attitude toward drug abusers, as well as my job at the police department, opened a new, exciting outreach for me. During the summer my friends at church told me about various acquaintances who had gotten involved in drugs or alcohol. One day I met fifteen-year-old Crystal. We talked for several hours. Seeing my interest and concern for her, she admitted she was involved with drugs and other drug users. I explained how Christ could change her life.

"But I've tried to stop taking drugs," she said, "and I can't do it."

"Look, Crystal," I said, "The Bible says that people who become Christians become brand new persons inside. The Lord can make it possible for you to give up drugs!"

Finally it dawned on Crystal that perhaps here was a way out. Bowing her head, she asked the Lord to forgive her and save her for Christ's sake.

Take my life completely, Lord, she prayed, *and help me to use it for You.* When she looked up, tears were streaming down her cheeks, but her face was radiant!

Crystal's letters to me since then have been full of joy. She has shared the Lord with her friends, and they now go to church with her. Four or five of them also accepted Christ into their lives.

"You know, I never respected my parents before," she wrote, "but now I really love them. Since I've received Christ, our relationship has improved greatly. Now our whole family rejoices together in the Lord, and we are held together in His love. Now we have a happy home!"

If the Lord hadn't opened my eyes, I probably never would have even spoken to Crystal. And since my attitude toward lost, young people has so greatly changed, the words of the great missionary, Amy Carmichael, have become especially meaningful to me: "If I can easily discuss the shortcomings and the sins of any; if I can speak in a casual way even of a child's misdoings, then I know nothing of Calvary love."

lights

JESSICA INMAN

**Trust in the LORD with all your heart and lean
not on your own understanding; in all your ways
acknowledge him, and he will make your paths straight.**

PROVERBS 3:5-6 NIV

"IT IS A MISTAKE TO LOOK TOO FAR AHEAD. ONLY ONE LINK IN THE CHAIN OF DESTINY MAY BE HANDLED AT A TIME."

—Sir Winston Churchill

I press the last push-pin into the wall. I am daringly/foolishly perched on my toes on my swiveling desk chair, arranging some white Christmas lights into a lattice formation above my closet door. Some events in my life in the last few months—my birthday and college graduation, among other things—have precipitated several greeting cards from special people, and I want to display them in my room in a creative fashion.

Hopping back on the chair after retrieving the cards, I begin sliding them between the lights and the wall; some of them I leave open to reveal the words of kindness and encouragement scrawled on the inside. Upon completion, the space of wall above my closet is a visual patchwork—little squares of handwriting, an ice cream cone, a dog with a hologram bone above his sleepy head.

When I plug in the lights, the cards illuminate and sparkle.

With a sigh I ponder, *Is there something wrong with me because I don't know exactly what I should do next with my life?*

I graduated from college in May with absolutely no idea what I was going to do the following week. With a hodgepodge of skills and a sense of passion sketchy at best, I tried out many different options throughout the summer. I felt pulled toward compassionate ministry, youth ministry, and writing in some capacity or another, but I didn't really know how to move forward or decipher a sense of "call" amid my own personal thoughts and desires.

Thus, I found the job hunt rather complicated. I developed a résumé, applied at a student mission's organization, and made some contacts within my denomination at a budding inner-city church in another part of the state. Meanwhile, I kept my comfy position as a youth pastor's secretary.

I interviewed at the inner-city church, and eventually landed an administrative assistant position with them and informed my boss that I would be leaving after September. I also sought counsel with an urban ministry leader in my own city, who warned me that if I plunged into urban work without clarity about God's purpose in my life, the road ahead could be very hard and possibly disastrous. Deciding to heed that warning, along with the war in my stomach over the whole affair, I declined the position only a few days before I was scheduled to move.

My last day as youth group secretary just happened to be the day after the publication of my first article. My boss insisted upon taking me to lunch that day; I consented. I walked into the restaurant and thought, *Wow, the whole church office staff decided to come to lunch at the same restaurant,* not realizing this was my going away/congratulations party.

I received a card signed by the staff, a few very sweet gifts, some kudos on my article, and a bowl of baked potato soup. This was Friday; on Monday, I would have no job.

I told my boss I'd continue to help him out a little bit during the interim—they hadn't found my replacement yet, and I was happy to help him while I continued to look for something with more hours each week.

In the end, I found myself without much direction, and ended up rejoining the staff at the church permanently. To pay bills I continued to write and otherwise try to make money however I could. As much as the office staff had wished me well when I "left," they welcomed me back with even more warmth.

Looking at the spread of cards on my wall again, I surveyed the warm wishes and read some of the inscriptions. Gloria had written on my good-bye card, "What a beautiful young woman of God you are—both inside and out! I am really going to miss you!" On my birthday card, Mollie had written, "Your metamorphosis into adulthood has been a joy to behold." Daleen scripted, "You deserve every wonderful graduation moment." And then there was Bryan. I got a little misty-eyed reading what he—someone I had admired and sometimes felt like I had failed—admired about me.

I stood under the lights and thought; *these people really seem to love me, and I don't think I understand that.*

I could tolerate lack of direction in other people. It made perfect sense to me that other people my age might struggle a little in figuring out what they were created to do the first year or two after college. But in myself, I expected more, and it was difficult to accept the seemingly aimless direction of my life. I was thoroughly perplexed by these short messages of love and belief from my coworkers. Perplexed, but grateful, and deeply conscious of the security God has given me through these people. Feeling their love, I can press on bravely, maybe making a couple of mistakes, but knowing that things will turn out in the end because God has gifted me in certain ways and desires to guide my life. There is an unmistakable hope in feeling loved and appreciated, and understanding that this love comes ultimately from Someone who directs my very steps.

It's getting late and yes, I should get to bed. After all, who knows what tomorrow will bring, what steps God will beckon me to take toward my future! Stepping back, I unplug the Christmas lights, hesitate a moment, then plug them back in. I may leave them on all night.

God had a plan

RANDY PIKE

(as told to Muriel Larson)

As the heavens are higher than the earth,

so are my ways higher than your ways

and my thoughts than your thoughts.

ISAIAH 55:9 NIV

Why can't I move my legs? I wondered panicking. I strained again to move them. Nothing happened. Fears flooded my mind.

I'm only eighteen! I cried silently. *Will I be crippled for life?*

An internist came into my hospital room. "What's wrong with me?" I asked.

"We don't know," he admitted.

After he left, I lay there thinking. I loved sports. *Will I ever be able to play basketball...baseball...or football...again,* I worried. *Will I be able to follow my dream and become a pioneer in Alaska?*

While my class was graduating from high school, I was still in the hospital receiving various treatments and therapy. Finally I was able to hold a fork and feed myself, sit up in bed, brush my teeth, and comb my hair. But my legs were still paralyzed.

One day a minister came to visit me. He was friendly, but he didn't stay long. He knelt by my bed and put his hand on my right arm. "Randall," he said, "I believe this will work out for you." Then he prayed for me, after which he arose and left.

That one statement stirred something up inside of me. It instilled in me a desire I didn't fully understand at the time.

I was in the hospital for eight long months. One day a therapist came in and measured my legs. "What's this all about?" I asked.

"We're going to make braces for you," the therapist answered.

"I'm not going to need those things!" I exclaimed angrily. I refused to accept the possibility that I might be crippled for the rest of my life. But whether I wanted to or not, I needed to learn to walk with the help of braces and crutches.

When I was eventually released to go home, I felt very bitter. *What could I ever do in life? I was 19. What girl would ever take a second glance at me now?*

One day a man from the Tennessee Department of rehabilitation came to see me. "We have all kinds of courses that can give you training to help you find your way in life," he said. As he said that, pain ripped through my heart at the thought of not being able to do with my life as I had planned. He read through a list of job opportunities, and I chose a radio announcer.

After attending the Tennessee School of Broadcasting in Nashville, I became a sports announcer, newscaster, and disk jockey at a radio station in Springfield, Tennessee. My DJ program soon became the most popular on the station.

One of the first programs they gave me to work on was the Preacher's Hour on Sunday, on which every minister in town was given fifteen minutes. As I read over the log with a fellow announcer, he jokingly remarked, "Say, Randy, I see you're going to sign on this preacher, Loy Cook. Watch out for him. He's a religious nut. Don't let him get to you!"

Sunday morning I signed Loy Cook on, then went into the news room to attend to something else. I could hear Cook preaching on the parable of the sower. As I listened, I became so interested that I was almost late in getting back to the board to sign him off.

Several weeks later, while I was pulling records for the farm program, another announcer came in with Loy Cook and introduced him to me. The preacher put his hand on my shoulder and said, "Son, are you a Christian?" That struck me in my heart like a knife, and the records I held clattered to the floor.

I lowered my eyes and answered, "I don't know what I am." I had received Jesus Christ as my Savior when I was thirteen, but I also knew I wasn't living like a Christian.

Loy Cook helped me pick up the records, all the while talking about the program on Sunday. "You'll be with me then, won't you?" he asked. "I'd like you to listen to the broadcast."

Eventually Loy convinced me to attend his church. Then one evening he preached on the subject, "The harvest...is plenteous, but the laborers are few" (Matthew 9:37).

When an invitation hymn was sung, I swung forward on my crutches. "What do you want, Randy?" the preacher asked. I gave him a quick review of my spiritual life and then said, "I think I need to accept the Lord again."

"No, that isn't what you need," he answered. He read Romans 12:1 to me. "What you need to do is rededicate your life to Christ," he continued, "and present your body as a living sacrifice to God." So I did—crippled legs and all.

The next day when I went to work, I told my boss I had recommitted my life to Jesus Christ. "I don't want to drink and party with the other guys," I said. "I don't want to live that way any more."

He looked at me and exclaimed, "That Loy Cook got ahold of you, didn't he!"

"Well, it's not really him," I said. "It's Someone bigger than he is."

I was true to my word, and I no longer seemed to fit in. A few days later the boss came in and pitched my time card to me. "Fill it out," he said, "and get out of here. You're through." So after a year at the station, I was out of a job.

Billy Gray, a friend at the station, came over to me and laid his hand on my shoulder. "Randy, you're making the biggest mistake you ever made," he said. "You have a career in this. You'll be sorry."

I finished filling out the time card and then shook hands with my friend. "Billy, I don't know everything yet," I said, "but I know this is right. And I'll be praying for you, that one day you will allow God to open your eyes to the truth as He has opened mine."

After I left the station, I went to work in a factory. I began preaching and sharing about my experience with Christ on the streets and in jails. My church later ordained me as a minister.

At a tent meeting one night someone introduced me to a lovely Christian girl named Addien, to whom I found myself very attracted. To my surprise, she seemed to like me, too, in spite of my handicap. In fact, we fell in love; and when I proposed, she quickly accepted.

After we were married, I started a church. When that became self-supporting, I started one in another town. When that one was thriving, we went to Australia as missionaries and started a church there.

On our first furlough home in the States I learned that my friend, Billy Gray, had become a Christian and had also started preaching the gospel. "Those words you said to me at the radio station were what did it," Billy told me. Billy is not only a preacher, but he now owns the radio station from which I was fired!

That minister in the hospital had been right. God did have a plan for my life. And His plan has been more fulfilling and far more rewarding to me than anything I could have ever imagined in this life and the life to come!

anything is possible

JENNIFER JOHNSON

"With God all things are possible."

MATTHEW 19:26 NKJV

Anticipation gripped and knotted my stomach. My knees swished back and forth like Jell-O on a plate. The cool October wind whipped my hair and smacked my cheeks.

"Go, go." Mrs. Maupin motioned for the troop of high school seniors and their escorts to trek the football field.

Sweat, popcorn, and perfume from one of the girls warred for victory of my senses. The knot in my stomach worked its way through my diaphragm and into my throat. Jack Frost swished around my panty-hosed legs sending a chill to the end of my toes. For years I had dreamed of this moment. Years.

> "IT'S THE GREATEST SHOT OF ADRENALINE TO BE DOING WHAT YOU'VE WANTED TO DO SO BADLY. YOU ALMOST FEEL LIKE YOU COULD FLY WITHOUT THE PLANE."
>
> —Charles Lindbergh

My stepdad locked his arm with mine. "You look pretty, Jennifer." His worn and a bit out-dated, wool sports coat provided much needed warmth, and I leaned closer to him. Uncertainty had birthed a great irony, for I had always felt awkward around my mother's second husband. But, today...today, his presence gave me great comfort and relief.

I smiled. "I don't know about that."

A blast of frigid air dashed my cheeks, and I gripped my stepdad's arm tighter. I lowered my head to ward off the winter wind. Only days before, nature's carpet had been lush, a warm, soft pillow to our acrobatic falls during cheerleading practice. Today however, the grass crunched like broken icicles beneath my much-too-worn black pumps. "Can you believe it's this cold?"

My stepdad chuckled. "Yeah, It's probably good Grandma couldn't come both weekends. It's too cold for her."

My heart sank.

Grandma, the most precious person in my universe, wouldn't be a viewing participant to my five minutes of fame. My moment. Well, in truth, no one had vowed this to be my moment. In fact, twenty-six of us vied for this esteemed honor. For all I knew, the moment belonged to someone else. I sighed. Still, I longed for my grandma's presence in the crowd.

Closing my eyes, I took a deep breath and exhaled. My nerves were getting the best of me.

Albert wouldn't be in attendance either.

Sadness enveloped my spirit. Drill sergeants didn't normally allow privates to skip a day of basic training for an evening with their girlfriends. My special moment was no exception. Only my mom, step dad, two brothers, and a sister would witness the event. I glanced at my mom, camcorder in hand, and grinned. My little sister waved and pointed at my step dad and me. I winked and waved back.

"Welcome to Madison Southern's..." The announcer's deep voice boomed over the speakers.

I froze.

"Third runner-up is Ms. Kimberly Shouse. She is escorted..."

I looked up at the announcer, and then scanned the bleachers again. The cheerleaders jumped up and down, yelling, encouraging, and congratulating one of our teammates. Teachers and parents smiled and applauded. There were so many fans.

"Second runner-up, Ms. Valerie..."

Heartless claps brought my hands together, then apart, together, then apart. *God please let him call my name next. This means so much to me. What if he doesn't call my name? Please, let me be next.*

"First runner-up, Ms. April Ramsey..."

Okay, that was it. My plastered smile had cracked. Forcing my hands to meet again, I clapped heartlessly for my friend. Only one slot remained unfilled, and some twenty of us stood in the middle of the field.

My step dad leaned toward me. "It's you, Jennifer. It's you." I wanted to scream at him. How could he taunt me like that? He didn't understand how important this was to me.

"No, it's not me." I swallowed back tears.

"Yes, it is. It's you. It's you."

In a way, I felt flattered that he was trying to make me feel better. As rocky as our relationship had always been, it was kind of nice to have him cheering me on.

"And, the 1990 Madison Southern Homecoming Queen is..."

Why couldn't he just say it? Why couldn't he just get it over with? Prolonging the agony of defeat was torturous.

"...Ms. Jennifer Collins."

What? What did he say? I tried with everything in me to replay the words the man had just spoken. *Whose name was that?*

"I told ya." My step dad released my arm and began a chorus of clapping.

Tears of joy spilled down my cheeks. Cupping my hand over my mouth, I walked excitedly, proudly, blissfully toward my court of princesses. And, I was their queen. Me–Jennifer Collins—the girl who had to work every free evening at Long John Silver's to pay for cheerleading, clothes, make-up, and haircuts had been chosen. Me—the girl who had to borrow Mrs. Tyree's teal suit to wear this evening. The gal whose family used food stamps and lived in a shack, whose home life was anything but bliss—that girl had won.

Mrs. Maupin stepped forward and placed the rhinestone crown atop my head. Mrs. Sills handed me a dozen long-stemmed roses. I clutched the bouquet to my chest and sniffed the invigorating fragrance of…endless opportunities. Because, that night I learned that life is bigger than our circumstances. With steadfast trust in God and belief in ourselves, anything is truly possible.

a standing ovation

CANDY ARRINGTON

"Therefore, since we are surrounded by such a great cloud of witnesses, let us throw off everything that hinders... and let us run with perseverance the race marked out for us."

HEBREWS 12:1

Like most high school students, graduation was her goal. But Ginger Schrieffer was not like most high school students. Ginger was dying.

During junior high school, Ginger began experiencing some coordination and motor skill difficulties. After a series of tests, she was diagnosed with Hallervorden-Spatz, a rare motor neuron disease similar to Amyotrophic Lateral Sclerosis—Lou Gehrig's disease. Hallervorden-Spatz is characterized by progressive weakness in the muscles of the arms and legs. There is no known cure for the disease.

By the time Ginger entered tenth grade she was wheelchair-dependent. Because of her disability, there were several education options available to her: homebound schooling, a reduced class load which would stretch her time in high school by several years, or continuing on a regular schedule despite obvious obstacles.

From the beginning of her battle with this disease, Ginger adopted Isaiah 40:31 (NIV) as her life verse. "Those who hope in the LORD will renew their strength. They will soar on wings like eagles, they will run and not grow weary, they will walk and not be faint." This verse gave her the drive and determination not only to strive toward high school graduation, but also to graduate with her class. Ginger showed tremendous courage with this goal, and her high school committed to match her determination. By installing ramps, granting elevator privileges, adapting bathroom facilities, assigning wheelchair "pushers," allowing her to dictate written assignments, use of a tape recorder in lecture classes, and provision of textbooks on tape, the school helped Ginger toward her goal.

Somehow the wheelchair wasn't as noticeable once Ginger's coppery curls, crystal blue eyes, and engaging smile came into view. Her zest for life was evident, and her magnetic personality drew people to her despite the handicaps. Ginger had a multitude of friends from all areas: church, school, and community.

When times were hard, Ginger clung to the words of Philippians 4:11-12, "I have learned to be content whatever the circumstances....I have learned the secret of being content in any and every situation." She didn't just eek her way through high school. Ginger involved herself fully in all aspects of it.

Her love of music resulted in singing and traveling with the high school chorus. Ginger was part of a "lunch bunch" that sat together everyday. This group, made up of friends from church, made sure Ginger always had a place at the table. Homeroom president and football star, Brian Smith, waited each morning in the hall for Ginger, who always seemed to be running late, and raced her to homeroom just before the tardy bell rang. A highlight of her senior year was her selection by the student council as "student of the week." She enjoyed all the activities associated with this honor.

While entering the elevator one morning, Ginger was joined by injured football star, Erik Neely. As he maneuvered his wheelchair in beside hers, Erik teased, "It took a game injury for me to have the privilege of sharing the library elevator with you." It was then that Ginger learned the football coach had used her as an example in a pre-game pep talk. "I want you men to play with the determination and courage that we see in that girl in the wheelchair," said the coach.

Ginger quietly made an impact on those around her, often without even realizing it. Her overarching goal, in addition to high school graduation, was to teach children. This goal was fulfilled at church and in the community. As a part of a therapy swim group at the Y.M.C.A., Ginger was asked to help with and be an example for children in the program. She especially connected with a four-year-old boy with cerebral palsy. It was not unusual to see Ginger feeding this four-year-old or a stroke victim on the days the therapy group went out to lunch or celebrated someone's birthday. Years later, she herself would have to be fed by another.

Amazingly, Ginger never tired of giving to others. She saw beyond her own disabilities and always had a desire to help others when it would have been easy to feel sorry for herself instead.

She had a reputation as a prayer warrior and was often asked by students and adults alike to intercede for them. She identified with and listened to the problems of others. These qualities in Ginger inspired a church youth discipleship group to select her as their "Number One World Changer," awarding her with a visit and an autographed T-shirt.

Like most girls, Ginger looked forward to her senior prom. She selected a dress, had her thick copper curls styled, carefully applied her make-up, and looked stunning for the evening. Her brother-in-law, Brian, was her escort. As he gently lifted her from her wheelchair and supported her, she "danced" for brief moments with her classmates. Friends gathered around Ginger with cameras, snapping treasured group pictures. On that evening, Ginger was no different than any other girl at the prom.

Despite the daily hurdles of failing muscles, a verse that kept a smile on Ginger's face and spread joy to everyone was Nehemiah 8:10. "This day is sacred to our Lord. Do not grieve, for the joy of the Lord is my strength." Her steady faith in God and reliance on his strength were an encouragement to those around her.

Ginger overcame the obstacles one day at a time. Sometimes those obstacles came in the form of gagging on her food if she laughed while eating. Sometimes it was the tediousness of extra equipment and aids to enable her to do routine activities. Other times her independence surfaced as she tried to make it from one place to another without help. On one occasion her wheelchair rolled down a hill too fast and tipped over, resulting in scraps and bruising. But each new day became a part of a journey bringing her one step closer to her ultimate goal.

When graduation night finally arrived, there was an air of celebration. The finish line was within sight. When Ginger's name was called, she accepted her diploma with great pride and a wide smile. The crowd spontaneously rose to their feet, accompanied by thunderous applause. Ginger had done it. With the help of God, her family, and friends, Ginger had won a victory over her disease. Once the ceremony was over Ginger was swarmed by family and friends. It was truly a night to celebrate.

Several years later, the progress of her disease became rapid. Even at this stage, Ginger continued to pray daily through a prayer list with her mother. In these last days of her life, she remained actively involved in ministry to others.

Ginger's final months were spent in a recliner in the room especially designed for her which overlooked a sparkling lake. Although she couldn't speak, her eyes continued to communicate her zest for life and her undaunted spirit.

Her funeral was a joyous celebration of her life, her love for God, her family, her church, and her friends. There were tears, but overwhelmingly they were tears of joy. Once again, those who loved her offered a standing ovation with their words as they ushered Ginger into the presence and protection of her loving heavenly Father.

Upon her graduation to eternal life, I am confident Ginger again received a standing ovation from a great cloud of witnesses and a "well done, good and faithful servant" from God the Father.

flying solo

CINDY THOMSON

Commit your way to the LORD; trust in him and he will do this:
He will make your righteousness shine like the dawn,
the justice of your cause like the noonday sun.

PSALM 37:5-6 NIV

I remember the third time I graduated. It was a sweltering day in June in the basketball arena of a local university—not the one I was graduating from, however. At the time, Wright State University did not have a suitable facility and so they rented space from another university in town. My high school graduation had taken place in that same arena. I had opted not to attend my second graduation from a local community college.

Because of some indecision on my part, it was six years after my high school graduation, rather than four, before I earned my bachelor's degree. I had looked forward to this, my third graduation. I wanted to be a teacher, a very good teacher, so I

"WHAT IS THE RECIPE FOR SUCCESSFUL ACHIEVE-MENT? TO MY MIND THERE ARE JUST FOUR ESSENTIAL INGREDIENTS: CHOOSE A CAREER YOU LOVE.... GIVE IT THE BEST THERE IS IN YOU.... SEIZE YOUR OPPORTU-NITIES.... AND BE A MEMBER OF THE TEAM."

—Benjamin F. Fairless

studied hard, receiving better grades at my university than I had ever received before. I was graduating that day with honors.

There were thousands of people there, including a delegation from Japan. Apparently they had arrived to learn about higher education in the United States and had included Wright State in their study. Since their arrival coincided with graduation, they were invited to attend and given an opportunity to speak to the crowd. I don't remember who they were or what they said, only that they spoke in Japanese and an interpreter was required. As the speeches droned on, sweat tricked beneath my black robe, threatening to saturate my new dress.

Even though I had received my degree months earlier, I was determined to take part in the graduation ritual. I looked forward to being publicly recognized for my hard work. But now, as the day grew warmer, I questioned my decision. *Was it really necessary to sit through such an ordeal?* I glanced up to the rows of stadium seats. *What was my family doing up there? Fidgeting? Running to the concession stand for beverages?*

The sound of applause woke me from my self-absorbed thoughts. The oration was over. Now we could get on with the process of handing out a multitude of college diplomas. The president of the university took the podium, apparently to announce the first college's awards. It wouldn't be the college of education, I realized. We were seated in the back. The enormous college of science and engineering would probably go first.

"Thank you, thank you." He bowed to the overseas guests. "And now for our commencement speaker."

I had forgotten that the Japanese visitors were not the scheduled key speakers. *How long would this take?* I rubbed the starched neck of my robe and twisted in my molded plastic chair.

"Mike Peters is an accomplished cartoonist. After serving in Vietnam, Mike landed a position as cartoonist at the Dayton Daily News in 1969. Since that time his political cartoons have appeared in numerous publications both nationally and internationally. Just last year he was awarded the Pulitzer Prize for journalism."

I admit my interest was peaked. I had read his work and thought it was quite funny. But what could a cartoonist have to say to my graduating class?

Mr. Peters took the podium. After his preliminary thank yous and his courteous remarks to the visiting guests, he began to talk about his career journey.

"I was always a dreamer, sketching my ideas on every available piece of paper, even in the margins of my school work. Teachers hate that. One of my teachers told me, 'Mike, you have to pay attention in class. You can't draw cartoons for the rest of your life.'"

Mike Peters continued to give examples in his life of how he never gave up his dream. He was driven to follow the gift he'd been given, despite what others might think. He could have given up, followed a more traditional path. But he didn't because the artist within him would not allow that.

He was funny, articulate, and timely in his comments to the class. Suddenly, walking across a stage in front of everyone to receive an envelope from my college dean did not seem so vital. What was most important was what I would do after that day.

I'll never forget, even two decades later, the gift Mike Peters gave us, the graduates of Wright State University, that day. In the envelope with the diplomas was a drawing from Mike Peters of the Wright Brothers standing in front of their plane. Above the clouds were the words, "Good luck. It's your turn to fly solo!"

I'm not an artist, and neither were many others who graduated that day. But the message was clear. Whatever gift you've been given, you're the only one who can use it in the way God intended. The Wright Brothers didn't give up their dream, and look what that dream has transformed into today. Mike Peters didn't give up his dream either, and he's achieved professional success and recognition. Once someone graduates, it's his or her turn—to fly, write, heal, nurture, encourage, build, create, and serve.

I still have that cartoon from Mike Peters, and I continue to remind myself that God created me with specific talents. This graduation was not an ending, but rather a beginning. Now, I truly look at things with a new perspective. Each day I try to remember to commit my life plans to His care, knowing that if I do, I'll succeed.

the unexpected miracle

AMY ALLEN

(as told to Esther M. Bailey)

To him who is able to do immeasurably more than all
we ask or imagine...to him be glory...in Christ Jesus.

EPHESIANS 3:20-21 NIV

Wow! God really did it up big! It had never entered my
mind to ask Him for a full-tuition scholarship to college, but
when I read the letter, I felt like God had carved my name on
His latest miracle.

At the same time I realized the price that had been paid for
my joy. The Bible college was offering the scholarship in honor of
the ministry of a man I had called Grandpa before he died, and
Grandma Frick had chosen me to receive the memorial grant.
Even in death Grandpa was there for me as he had been in life.

Ever since I can remember, Grandma and Grandpa Frick were part of my life. My real grandparents lived in different cities, but the Fricks were always nearby. They were my Christian role models as well as my adopted grandparents.

I looked back at what God had already done for me and wondered what He had in store for my future. Growing up in the church, I had always done Christian things. I asked Jesus to come into my heart as soon as I knew I should. It wasn't until I was in the eighth grade that I realized I needed something more. I was really down on myself—to the point that I even considered suicide. *What do I have to live for?* I kept asking myself. *I'm ugly, and I'm tired of being called a "Jesus freak" or a "church girl."*

When my dad sensed that something was terribly wrong, we had a talk. Dad listened and then told me, "Name some things you do like."

I answered with the first things that popped into my mind: "Sunsets...dolphins."

"Amy, you know that if you died today you could never see another sunset. You'd never see the dolphins that you've always wanted to see." Dad reminded me that life is good even during the toughest of times, and he pointed out the words of Scripture. The verse that made the greatest impression on me was Psalm 139:14: "I praise you because I am fearfully and wonderfully made." I didn't need to feel bad about myself because God "doesn't make trash."

For the first time I realized how much I needed Christ to walk with me every day of my life. I wanted to serve God with all of my heart, all of my mind, and all of my soul, so that I would be totally focused on Him.

My struggles didn't go away, but I had Someone to share them with. During my freshman year of high school, the school seemed so big that I just sort of faded into the background. I didn't do the kind of stuff other kids were doing; so I didn't fit in with the crowd. My youth group at church was what kept me going.

I moved several times during the early part of high school. Every time I moved, the kids would invite me to a party. I always explained, "No, I don't drink," and then they would ask me why. When I said, "I'm a Christian," that cooled almost all possible friendships.

During my last two years of high school, I started incorporating my Christian witness into my school papers. In English, we were asked to write about the most important thing in life. I wrote about my relationship with God. Teachers sometimes cause trouble for kids who stand up for God, but my teachers didn't.

Finally, guys started asking me out—gorgeous guys that all the girls dreamed over. But I turned them down because I knew they weren't right for me.

I stood true to my standards all through high school, but it would have been so easy to fall into a trap. I had a lot of lonely nights because I wouldn't go to parties and go out with guys. A lot of times I wanted to give up and say, *Forget it. This Christian thing is too much work.* Thank God that I didn't!

I dated a few guys in my youth group at church. Most of the dates I went on were casual, but I did have a few serious relationships. We did a lot of things with groups because we didn't want to let down our guard.

One of my biggest struggles came right after high school graduation. Most everyone who was close to me moved away—including my boyfriend and several good friends. Even my sister was gone for a good part of the summer. I was frustrated about college. I knew that I wanted to make something of myself. For the previous two years I had worked at Dairy Queen, and I knew I didn't want to do *that* the rest of my life! Bible college was too far away and cost too much; so I figured I'd just go to a community college.

Then the scholarship came, and I was totally amazed. It was as though God had opened the door and shoved me right through! I could see how He had prepared me to leave home by slowly pulling my friends and causing me to rely on Him. During my time alone I had learned to depend upon God instead of people. And I treasured my time with Him more than anything else.

College with Christian friends will be great. I suppose I'll have struggles there, too, but I'm too excited to get concerned about that right now. Being "a good girl" hasn't always been easy, in fact, it's been hard at times. But without a doubt it's been worth it. I now walk with a lot of self-confidence and my head held high. I'm proud to be where I am. When I get discouraged I'll just hang in there and remember God has always been there for me and will continue to always be there.

dreams really do come true

NANCY B. GIBBS

He guards the paths of justice and protects those who are faithful to him. Then you will understand what is right, just, and fair, and you will know how to find the right course of action every time.

PROVERBS 2:8-9 NLT

The day I fell in love with my husband, Roy, he shared his heart with me. He explained how he had always wanted to become a teacher. Once he began his college career, however, he lost sight of his goal. He received a diploma, but hadn't taken the courses that he needed to obtain his teaching certificate. I sensed that he regretted the decision he had made long before he met me.

Right then and there, I decided that I was going to marry Roy. I also decided to help him reach his lifelong goal. A couple of months later, we became husband and wife. Getting married was the easiest part of the plan. The more difficult part of the strategy was still before us.

Six years sped by. I realized by the expression on his face each autumn, the career my husband wanted more than anything else was to teach school. After having his transcript evaluated, we discovered that he would have to attend the university for approximately eighteen months before he could secure his teaching certificate. We couldn't come even close to being able to afford the tuition.

Our youngest child was entering the first grade that year. For the first time in a long time I would have free time on my hands. I decided to search for a job to enable me to pay Roy's tuition and purchase the books needed for his classes. I glanced through the classified advertisements in the newspaper but didn't see anything that interested me.

I remembered however, a conversation with a friend from home a few years prior, who had told me about the university my husband wanted to attend offering free tuition for their employees. In addition, the employee's immediate family members could attend tuition-free. I put on a business suit and went to the university to apply.

I walked into the personnel office, filled out an application, and took a typing test. A little while later, I returned home. As I walked in the front door, my telephone rang.

"Would you please come back to meet with our personnel manager," the secretary at the university asked.

"Sure," I replied. "I will be there shortly."

During the conversation with the personnel manager, she asked me why I wanted to work at the university. I explained how my husband's dream was to become a teacher. She smiled. Before I left her office, she assured me that an appropriate position would be found for me.

Our entire family rejoiced as I shared the news with my husband that evening. The kids cheered. Roy smiled brightly, while asking a hundred questions.

Shortly, I began working at the university, and Roy began getting ready to return to school. To make ends meet, we both worked multiple jobs while Roy attended school. The kids helped out at home. They didn't complain about the extra efforts they had to put forth. They, too, knew how important Roy's dream was to him.

A few months later, I received a notice that the university benefits were changing. Roy would have to pay for his tuition. We didn't have the money to pay the cost of the private school. I cried when I had to break the news to Roy. We weren't giving up on Roy's dream that quickly, however.

We went to see the president of the university. After we told him how hard we were working to make Roy's dream come true, he understood our dilemma and signed a form stating that Roy could finish his degree tuition-free.

When Roy walked down the center-aisle to receive his diploma, I was beyond elated. It felt as though our entire family was graduating from college. With God's help, we had completed the plan made on the very day that I fell in love with my husband. He began teaching a few weeks later and has taught school now for twenty years.

I often look back and wonder what we would be doing if we hadn't decided to look to God for direction. After a few years on the job, Roy won the countywide teacher of the year award. He has touched the lives of hundreds of young people over the last two decades.

God's way is not always easy. Success is possible, however, when we depend on God to lead, guide, and direct us through our plans, goals, and dreams. For with God, dreams really do come true.

the moustache and my father

MICK THURBER

**Honor your father and your mother, that your days may be
long upon the land which the LORD your God is giving you.**

EXODUS 20:12 NKJV

To say my father and I didn't get along would be putting it
mildly. We seemed so different, so far apart, during my high
school years. I can hardly recall a kind word spoken between us.
We fought constantly. I considered him my enemy because he
was too strict and put limitations on me that none of my friends
had to endure at their homes. We could barely tolerate each
other. I resented almost everything about him. He didn't
understand me nor seem the least bit interested in getting to
know me. He wasn't proud of me, the way most fathers are of
their sons, and I could never recall a single time that my dad told
me he loved me.

Truth is, I never gave my dad much of a chance to get close to me. I pushed him away, turning a deaf ear when he would give me advice or guidance, refusing him the opportunity to express his love toward me. We hardly spoke to each other, and when we did, the conversation was usually laced with words of bitterness, hatefulness, and cursing. I'm sure he could see in my eyes the resentment and lack of respect I held for him. My daily goal was simply to avoid any contact with him. I figured if we didn't see each other, we wouldn't fight. It must have hurt him terribly. I didn't know I was breaking his heart, and in the process, my mother's.

I thought a lot about my closest friends and the relationships they had with their fathers. How easy it appeared to be for them. They actually seemed to like each other. They would talk of spending time together doing all the fun things fathers and sons do. When the subject of parents came up, they didn't trash their dads, the way I did mine.

As much as I pretended that this all didn't bother me—it did. It was like a vast, empty hole in my life.

With all the bad blood between us, I never took the time to notice that Dad worked incredibly hard at his job, year after year, to provide for our needs—three meals a day, a nice house to live in, a car to drive. He was there for me anytime I was sick and needed to visit the doctor or take a trip to the emergency room. He even helped me deliver newspapers on my daily newspaper route every Sunday morning when the papers were huge. Free of charge. I never had to ask him. He was just always there; ready to help at 4:30 A.M. every Sunday morning. I never appreciated these things or thanked him like I should. I didn't realize it then, but my dad was actually the best friend I had.

It was mid-summer. I had just graduated high school and enrolled in college for the fall semester, and my life was about to change.

One Sunday evening, I agreed to go with some friends to a church service to hear a young preacher and his Christian rock band. Everyone seemed excited about it so I went along. We sat near the front and listened as the band played and the preacher offered the familiar message about a loving God and His desire to save people like me from their sins and give to them eternal life. I had gone to this church several times during my high school years, and it seemed I had heard this sermon many times before. But on this night, as if for the first time, I was confronted by this preacher's piercing question, "Have you ever given your life to Jesus Christ?"

All at once I realized my meager attempts at being religious meant nothing and that my account with God was not settled. I was so overtaken with conviction that I whispered to the person next to me, "I've never done this before. I've never given my life to God." For the next few minutes, with my head bowed, I examined my life that was now so obviously empty and determined to answer God's invitation immediately. That night I gave my life to Christ the best I knew how. I was made right with Him. He transformed my heart, and I was forever changed.

For the next several weeks I discovered things were different. Now, the Bible had real meaning and significance to me. I understood it was God's Word to me and that it applied to my life everyday. My friends seemed different. My job was different. My family was different. I began to understand it wasn't entirely my dad's fault for our dysfunctional relationship—it was largely mine. I now could see that it was my disobedience and lack of respect that drove the wedge between us. And I knew in my heart that God wanted me to change. It was perfectly clear that God wanted my relationship with my father to be restored and that it had to start with me.

What was I to do? How could I be different around my dad? How could I change the years and years of war between us? Could I truly honor him after all we'd been through? How would he respond to my change of heart? I didn't know the answers to these questions, but somehow I knew God could take care of it.

So, with all my heart, I committed our relationship to God and prayed He would give me a new start with my father.

Not knowing exactly how to begin, I determined the least I could do was show respect to my father and simply obey him.

The thought of unquestioned obedience was hard for me to even imagine. Here I was—18 years old, with my friends all moving forward to new levels of independence, while I moved forward to a different kind of level, simply learning to obey my dad when he told me to do something—with no complaining, no excuses, no delays—just obedience, pure and simple. It was a little humbling. I'm sure my dad was a little leery at first with my new actions. He probably wondered if I had bumped my head or was going to hit him up for a new car or something.

Actually, these acts of obedience were not that hard at all. The simple things, like taking out the trash, helping around the house and responding positively when I was told "No," took on a whole new meaning. I could see this was God's way for me. It felt good to do the things I was asked to do. It seemed I was finally growing up to be the son my dad always wanted and I had always wanted to be. And I loved it! This was amazing! I found that I was actually looking forward to opportunities to obey my dad. It gave me a real sense of joy because I knew it pleased him and I knew it pleased God.

Over the next few months God made some real changes between me and my father. I was surprised one day when dad asked me to go to the grocery store with him, just to ride along. Try to imagine this—me and my dad—hanging out, talking, laughing, and becoming buddies! Just like everybody else. It was a miracle! God was truly blessing my life through this decision to follow Him.

Life was good. This "instant obedience—no matter what" thing was my new modus operandi. I'm not saying I was perfect and always did the right thing. I struggled and messed up on many occasions, but God was always there to help me.

It was during my sophomore year of college that I encountered my biggest challenge for obedience.

It came shortly after a major accomplishment—I had grown my first moustache. *What a beautiful upper lip,* I thought to myself as I carefully combed and shaped this new addition to my face. I had convinced myself that this little strip of hair below my nose looked so good that it was going to be a permanent fixture.

One evening after school I had decided to hang out with some friends (at the time I was living at home and working my way through school). I had gotten dressed and was leaving when I walked past my father on the way out of the house. He gave me a funny little smile and said, "Son, I wish you would shave that ol' moustache off." I paused for a moment and sort of acknowledged his request and then proceeded on toward my car. *Why should he care about my moustache? What business is it to him?* I wondered. *Why would he ask me to shave? He knows how much I like my moustache.* But then the thought of my commitment to obey hit me like a brick. *Did Dad tell me to shave it off? Lord are you wanting me to shave my moustache off? No, surely not.* Dad just said, "I wish you would shave it off." He didn't actually order me to.

So I reasoned with God and determined that if dad orders me to shave, I'll shave. But in my heart, I did not want to. I wanted to keep this hairy lip.

It couldn't have been more than two days later when I saw my dad again with that same smile and that same request, "Son, I wish you would shave that moustache. I think you would look better." I just glanced at him and didn't really say anything. I gave a half-hearted nod and made my way to the door. As soon as I got outside I prayed, *Now God, you know that if Dad will tell me directly to shave my moustache, I will. You know I will. But he is only saying, "I wish you would." God, I know this moustache situation is not a big deal, but I want to do the right thing, and that is a big deal.*

So for a few days I actually struggled over this issue of my "to be—or not to be" moustache. My commitment to obey—no matter what—was pressing me. I reasoned over and over why I shouldn't have to shave, but told God I would if He really wanted me to.

Finally, Dad mentioned one last time his desire for the moustache to go. I was perplexed. I was about to start again, the reasoning process with God, when He spoke to my heart very clearly. *Mick, what's the difference in your father wishing you to do something and ordering you to do something? There shouldn't be any difference. They require the same honor and obedience. You should do it simply because your dad desires it of you—and know it will please Me.*

So, without any further hesitation, I shaved off my moustache.

Just moments later, I was on my way out and again walked past my father. This time he just smiled without saying a word. In that quick exchange there was something that let me know he was pleased. I spent the evening with my friends and came home later that night. All the lights were out except for the lamp my parents kept on for me. They had already gone to bed, and as I quietly walked to my room I heard Dad say from behind his closed bedroom door, "Son, I need to talk to you."

So I cracked their door open. It was totally dark, and I couldn't see anything but black. "Did you lock the doors? Did you turn out all the lights?" he asked, as part of the nightly routine (I had it memorized). "Yes," I said. "Everything is taken care of. Good night." And as I was about to leave he said one last thing, "Son...I just wanted to tell you...that I love you."

I stood there frozen for a moment. The words, "I love you, too" trembled out of my mouth in a whisper.

For the first time that I can remember, my dad told me he loved me. I couldn't hold back my emotions. In that moment my heart was overwhelmed with thanks to God for doing a work in my life that I could never have done on my own. My dad and I had come full circle. To this day, it remains one of the greatest defining moments of my life. I will treasure it forever. And it all came about when a young guy in college decided to obey.

finish, and finish well

DARLA SATTERFIELD DAVIS

Do you not know that in a race all the runners run, but only one gets the prize? Run in such a way as to get the prize.

1 CORINTHIANS 9:24 NIV

My parents were both excellent students and made high marks in school. Their families could not afford to send them to college, and without the loans and grants we have today it was a near impossible dream for many. So they married young, began working, and raised a family.

When my brother and I were in grade school my mother began taking some night courses at a local High School. We thought it was so funny that our *mother* was going to school! What we did not know then, was that her great secret and sorrow was that she had never finished the last year of high school and did not have a diploma.

By nature, my mother is on the shy side. She grew up in a small town in Oklahoma, and then eventually moved to the big city lights of Southern California. A move like that must have been a little intimidating, to say the least. But the desire to finish school and get that diploma overcame any reservations she may have had.

My mother took a great deal of pride in her schoolwork, and I remember her writing pages and pages in her beautiful penmanship for her classes. Our lives did not change while she was in school, nor did the household suffer in the least as she continued her studies. It never occurred to us that anything was different, or that she was burning the midnight oil long after we had been tucked into bed.

What did get our attention was a newspaperman from "The Garden Grove Register" who came to our house to take pictures of us with our mother. She was graduating the following night as Valedictorian of her class!

I remember her fancy 1960's hairdo, the lavender suit, the smell of White Shoulders perfume, and the orchid corsage she wore. I thought she looked like a princess! I remember how proud we were of her, and all the attention she got that night.

Throughout my life, my parents both continued their pursuit of knowledge through college classes, seminars, and course studies. They made sure my brother and I had many learning opportunities by visiting museums, historical sites, and local places of interest.

Years later, when it was my turn to go back to school, I came across the statistics that showed the impact of a parent's educational level on the child. I was especially interested by how much more impact the mother's educational status seemed to have on the children, than the father's.

I thought back about my mother's graduation and how determined she was not only to finish, but to finish well. I have always been grateful for my mother's example and encouragement to continue in education. This is a value I have tried to encourage in my own daughter, as well as my students over the years. "Finish, and finish well."

circles

ASHLYN EVERETT

For You, O LORD**, will bless the righteous; with favor
You will surround him as with a shield.**

PSALM 5:12 NKJV

The glow from my alarm clock told me it was past time to be asleep. My eyes closed with heaviness, but my mind would not stop spinning. It ran in a million circles at once. I tried to push the thoughts away. I didn't understand how to organize them in my brain, and I couldn't grasp their beginning or ending. But, as I attempted to forget the situation, my brain raced with activity.

Do you understand what I am going through, God? I feel so overwhelmed, I feel so inadequate, I feel so weak, and I don't know what to do.

My brain tossed and turned in so many different ways during those several weeks; my head twisted in so many awkward scenarios; and tears streamed down my face from the confusion.

143

How do you lovingly disagree with and confront another believer? I just didn't know, and I was burdened with awareness that how I handled this situation would affect a lot of things at this stage in my life.

The job was perfect for me. Now out of high school and facing the challenge of paying for college; the job would fit my student lifestyle and paid well. My hard work had given me some mobility, as well. I had worked my way up to being probably the highest-paid young worker in the company, which was exciting. I knew the work would be long and hard, but I felt this job was where I needed to be. It was easy to step into my work situation this past summer with a willing spirit, just as I had each summer for five years.

One fruit season ended and transitioned to another in the middle of the summer, and so some of my duties changed as well. In the transition, I found myself being trained for a position as an employee supervisor, a new thing for me.

My supervisor trained me during the early part of July. As she named off the employees I would be in charge of, she briefly mentioned to me something that would change the whole course of my summer.

"See that girl? She is here on a student visa. She really doesn't have the right papers to work, though, so she is just working under a different name." I nodded my head as she explained this to me.

But my stomach did a little flop, and uneasiness started to arise in my mind.

God, is this right? I mean, I know she is not telling the truth by writing someone else's name on the schedule. But…this is probably not a big deal because she doesn't seem concerned about it.

I thought all Christians were supposed to have the same basic morals. So, I reasoned that my supervisor was probably right in what she was doing. After all, she was also my junior high Sunday school teacher, and her husband was a deacon in my church.

I took over most of the scheduling fairly quickly after my supervisor finished the training. I did not want to lie, but also felt it was my duty to honor my leader's decisions. So I did it. I scheduled the new girl under a different name. However, my conscience began to run circles around my thoughts.

God, I know that wasn't right. I shouldn't have lied to cover up anything. But,…putting her name down as somebody else's protects her and my supervisor as well. Maybe I am showing love to these people who have to deal with unjust laws.

At dinner that night, I talked over the situation with my brother. I just wasn't sure if I was right or if I was just making small things into a big deal. But after talking to him and my parents, and struggling through the situation, I concluded that I needed to address the issue with my supervisor. I even came to terms with the fact that I was willing to quit my job—the job that provided so perfectly for me to be a student—over the issue if needed.

The next day, I went to work with a headache and a knot in my stomach. As I drove to work, a song from Psalm 25 played on the radio. "No one whose hope is in you will ever be put to shame," ran the words.

Oh God, am I doing the right thing? My hope is in you Lord, and I trust you will guide me and not put me to shame.

I had a chance to talk to my supervisor about the situation that morning. She responded to me with surprise and some animosity. She saw the act of giving this girl a job as an act of Christian love. In her mind, love covered over the breaking of the law. My mind swayed a bit.

What if I really am not right about this whole situation? *God, you are a loving God, and I know I need to love people.*

But I stood firm in my decision not to schedule her under an assumed name. My supervisor finally agreed not to force me to cover up the indiscretion. The tension ran thick in the office for awhile—I just hoped the summer would pass quickly.

God, thank you for resolution. I don't like the conflict I feel with another Christian, but I pray you will continue to work on her heart.

I thought everything was resolved and completed—and all the worrying had come to end. And they had for a while. Until the end of the summer, when I found there was a possibility this same girl might be working under a different name again and without my knowledge. I was taken off guard. But I gathered all possible facts and went to talk to my supervisor again. I asked about the situation. Her response was immediately defensive. It was clear emotions ran high on both sides of the issue.

I was accused of not being loving. I was told I wasn't operating under God's standard. A higher law of love versus being "legalistic" was held over my head. I concluded that perhaps illegal things had not been occurring in the present situation as distinctly as in the first part of the summer, but I brought to light several other legal issues I felt weren't being addressed at the farm. These were moral oversights the company seemed to ignore for the sake of profits and inconvenience.

Our argument went on for several minutes, but I realized we were not in agreement on some fundamental issues. I left feeling defeated. I went back to my office and closed my door with tears threatening to spill over. In my emotional state, life looked bleak. There seemed to be no end to my mind's spinning circles. The confusion of what is right and wrong reigned in my heart. I felt the issues and arguments running around and around me.

God, I don't know what to do. My mind is a mess. Am I being legalistic? You do want me to love people, right? She was very angry with me, God. Maybe I did the wrong thing.

My head hurt—I just wanted to leave work and never come back. I left the office early.

Talking with my family and my pastor, I received conflicting advice. My pastor did not give me any conclusive answers, rather telling me to love and understand the perspective of my boss. I didn't know what to do. But I searched the Scriptures, and I poured out my thoughts in prayer.

What was the right thing to do? I could not think about anything except my conflict for several days. *When did Jesus allow people to break the law? And how could Christians whom I respect think in a way contrary to what I know as truth?*

Finally, I decided to write my supervisor a letter, explaining my position. I felt the overall position of the company was one that allowed employees to break the law in ways not agreeable or advantageous to the company. And ultimately, I decided I couldn't work for a company that allowed illegal dealings to take place.

I was a tangled ball of emotions the day I handed in my resignation letter. I struggled with quitting the security of my perfect out-of-school, need-the-money office job. I was giving up what I considered the security of having my school bills paid. But I let these things go with the letter.

I made my decision. I quit.

And with that decision came an undeniable peace, a true peace that was beyond all comprehension.

God has never failed me, and certainly I went on to complete my schooling. That summer, I learned the most valuable lesson of my life. God honored my decision to take the upright and honorable step. And I found that my provision was in God, not men, not a job or positions of esteem. But in God's way, I found a new level of meaning and blessing for my life.

you da man!

NANETTE THORSEN-SNIPES

**Your attitude should be the same that Christ Jesus had.
Though he was God, he did not demand and cling to
his rights as God. He made himself nothing; he took the
humble position of a slave and appeared in human form.**

PHILIPPIANS 2:5-7 NLT

While I desperately wanted my oldest son to go to college, I
knew, with three other mouths to feed and the mounting bills
from my early onset of arthritis, that it would have to wait.

I was more than proud, however, as he walked down the aisle
and accepted his high school diploma. I just didn't know how
he'd ever be able to get further than a waiter at a four-star
restaurant. But he did.

Over sandwiches and iced tea years later, I asked David how
he became so successful since he, his younger brother, and I had
done without so many things after my divorce in 1976.

With only secretarial skills I went to work as a part-time secretary—the only thing I could find during the recession of that year. The boys wore hand-me-downs, and we ate cheaply.

As the months passed, Christmas stared me in the face. I had little money and no friends or family nearby to help, so I bought two small gifts apiece for the boys, which was all I could afford.

Two weeks before Christmas, a friend brought us a tree, and I was eternally grateful; except the tree began to brown and shed. Two days before Christmas, all the browned needles lay on the carpet where we pricked our feet every time we passed it. Finally, David and I lugged the tree to the corner, and the three of us sat on yellow shag carpeting in front of a coffee table and opened gifts.

Years later, I looked at my son with pride. David was now the general manager of a prominent Atlanta hotel and successful beyond his imagination. As we munched chips, he began to relate a story I'd never heard.

"Let me tell you a story," he said. "Several years ago, I presented an orientation where I sat across from six of my newest employees. It was an informal orientation—time spent getting to know people and letting them get to know me and the hotel."

After a greeting and the usual statement of "Glad you're with us and part of the team," David opened the floor for questions.

"How did you get to where you are? I mean, how did you do it?" a housekeeper sitting in the back asked.

"Actually," he said, "it started when I was seven. My mother and father divorced, and Mom moved into an apartment. She sat me down one day and said, 'David, you're the man of the family now, and you have to come home from school, put your things up, and go next door to the neighbor's. You have to be a responsible, young man.'"

David smiled at the group. "I stepped up to that responsibility and learned how to get off the bus by myself and let myself into the apartment. Then, I went next door just as Mom said.

"Later, when I was fifteen, Mom took time to guide me into my first part-time job. It was one she thought suited my personality. I started as a busboy cleaning tables in a four-star restaurant dining room. I liked the restaurant business immediately and wanted to succeed, so I paid attention to people who made it to the top.

"We had a much-admired waiter team called George and Rick who made a lot of tips as waiters. I also noticed that their personal busboy made more tips than anyone else. So my goal became to work with George and Rick by being the very best busboy.

"I began bussing tables. Soon, I became the quickest and most efficient of all the busboys. Then I started carrying my own crumber, which sweeps a table of crumbs. I learned how to efficiently change a tablecloth without ever showing the table. Soon, George and Rick noticed my attention to detail and my desire to improve. They asked me to become *their* busboy.

"Since Rick, who was the back waiter, didn't like making Caesar salads tableside, I offered to take over. I learned how to make the best Caesar salads ever. Then I learned how to make desserts and talk in front of people so when Rick retired, George chose me to be the new back waiter.

"Then," said David to the spellbound group of new employees, "I became the best back waiter there was. I had to conquer the skill of delivering food. The bottom line was that I came into work every day and took responsibility by doing the very best I could."

"In time, I worked my way into doing presentations with George. By doing more and more of his job, I was rewarded by splitting George's gratuity fifty-fifty instead of receiving the usual fifteen percent.

"When George was promoted to Maitre de, I took his place and determined to be the best front waiter the restaurant had, learning more about food, drink, and decor.

"Step-by-step, I moved up the line, achieving almost everything I set my mind to do. From waiter to restaurant manager to marketing manager, nothing was impossible. I simply put my best effort into each new position."

As I listened to my son talk, I realized the more prominent David's position became, the more he remembered the "little" guy, something I instilled in him from my renewed walk with Jesus. I'm sure David remembered my reading the Bible where Paul said, "The entire law is summed up in a single command: Love your neighbor as yourself."

In my heart, I was thrilled to learn my son had remembered how Jesus Himself loved and mingled with people who were different from him.

David said he made an effort to eat lunch with the chef, asking how his day went. I was amazed how my son found the time to talk one-on-one with the doorman. And when he said he folded clothes with the housekeeping team while asking about their jobs, I almost clapped!

When a woman in the employee meeting squirmed in her chair and timidly raised her hand, David called on her. "Could I ask you a silly question?" she asked.

"Sure."

"I noticed your cufflinks. Those aren't your initials, are they?" she asked.

David glowed as he recalled his last day at his former job. "I'm glad you asked. No, those aren't my initials. When I left my last position, my assistant and employees gave me a light blue box from Tiffany's. I couldn't imagine what was in the box, but knowing my employees' sense of humor, I was prepared for anything."

"When I opened it, there were these silver cufflinks with the initials YDM. I knew I'd truly succeeded when all my employees shouted, 'David, you da man!'"

"I guess I better explain," he said. "When I first started work, my employees began repeating a catchy phrase whenever they saw me. 'You da man!' they'd shout. And I'd say, 'No, you da man!'"

"Every time one of my employees did something outstanding like bringing hot towels and a bottle of cold water for customers who'd been out running, I'd encourage them by saying, 'You da man!'"

As we prepared to leave our lunch meeting, I had a newfound respect for my son. I hugged David and whispered in his ear, "David, you da man!"

David continues to succeed because he loves people from all walks of life and accepts them just as they are. While David didn't make it to college, he graduated from the school of life, landing at the top of his profession. And all because he chose to live his life, God's way.

what are we doing tomorrow, Lord?

GLORIA CASSITY STARGEL

Commit thy way unto the LORD; trust also in him;

and he shall bring it to pass.

PSALM 37:5

"What's the matter?" my husband Joe asked as we sat at the dinner table. I felt pretty low.

The children would soon leave for college, and I was coming down with a recurring attack of Empty Nest Syndrome, complicated by a chronic case of Identity Crisis. Both of these maladies have similar symptoms: loneliness, sadness, depression, boredom, frustration, fatigue.

Joe suggested I go back to school, so I put the idea on the back burner of my mind to simmer.

I had always been a planner, a perfectionist, and a procrastinator. But that was before last year when I faced Joe's life-threatening illness. With the world crumbling at my feet I saw the futility of my plans. I began learning to trust God.

I earnestly wanted to trust Him in all areas of life. I wanted to find His will for me and to do it. But first I had to know who I was—to find me. The words of Saint Augustine express the yearnings of my heart, "Let me know Thee, Lord, and let me know myself."

In this new stance of learning to trust, now that the subject of college had come up, I asked God for guidance. His answer was not a gentle nudge, but a strong shove. All the right doors began to open unexpectedly; even a scholarship appeared.

I approached the first classes with fear and trembling. *Could I still think? Could I still learn?* After all, it had been twenty-seven years since I finished my freshman year. *Please Lord, don't leave me now,* I breathed.

And He didn't. I not only learned, but I enjoyed it. The young students were friendly, the faculty helpful. Oh, an occasional class made me feel invisible. Then there were times when I wished I *were* invisible. But I soon felt at home.

As days became weeks and weeks became semesters, the totally unexpected happened. College became, for me, a spiritual experience. One that changed me and my life completely. One that gave me the inner security I craved. The key, I think, was obedience.

The turning point came when, during my junior year, God directed me to study journalism. But for several months I doggedly continued my social work studies. Surely I had imagined God's message. *After all,* I argued, *I'm not a youngster anymore. What would I do with journalism?*

I'm so grateful that God didn't give up on me. I felt no peace until I finally went to my knees in surrender and changed my major field of study to journalism.

Upon my surrender, the Holy Spirit took control. It seemed the more I gave up my will to God's will, the more I felt the presence of the Holy Spirit. What joy to know He dwells within. "Now we have received, not the spirit of the world, but the spirit which is of God; that we might know the things that are freely given to us of God" (I Corinthians 2:12).

Looking back, I think I've always loved Jesus. Strange that I hadn't known He loves me. Even as a child I sang "Jesus Loves Me." I guess I thought "me" was a universal me. I found it difficult to realize God loves me—me, personally—me— imperfect Gloria. I mean, that is electrifying.

In his book, *Let God Love You,* Lloyd J. Ogilvie writes, "Obedience to our Lord is the continuous new beginning of unpredictable possibilities."

One such unpredictable possibility became reality for me when after three years on campus I graduated—suma cum laude! I floated down the aisle, oblivious to the crowd, the applause, the cameras. It was my day, and it was great.

More accurately—it was our day. Jesus stayed with me all the way. I feel He smiled that day at my childlike exuberance.

When fall came that year I actually missed campus life. Life is a thrilling adventure with God in control. Every day I wonder expectantly, *What are we doing tomorrow, Lord?*

the time between

SHARON HINCK

Peter answered him, "We have left everything to follow you!
What then will there be for us?"

MATTHEW 19:27 NIV

Shortly after my college graduation, an ugly thread slipped into my thoughts and coiled into a dark knot.

God owed me.

After all, I had prayerfully sought His direction during high school. I committed my life to full-time service for Him and chose a Christian college and a career of church youth work. Ted and I married during our junior year. With idealism equal to my own, my husband studied toward his degree as a minister of evangelism.

The sacrifices were real. Ted loaded UPS trucks at three in the morning before classes. I juggled a variety of odd jobs— babysitting, taking in typing, doing secretarial work on campus, and choreographing at a small local theater. We squinted over rewrites of papers, refined our class projects, and volunteered at local churches. We scrimped, struggled, and invented fifty different ways to make a baked potato serve as supper.

With each sparse meal or stressful test to study for, we remembered we were doing this for God. He was honing and preparing us for great work for His kingdom.

At last, we graduated.

Although I wouldn't have admitted it to a soul, I figured it was time for God to show His appreciation.

Ted and I filled out forms to proclaim our availability to serve a church in our denomination. In the tradition of our church body, we couldn't simply go job hunting. Ministry roles were filled by a church or school offering a "call." We specified our talents and skills, our desire to work in a large city, and our hope to serve together. The papers went out. We kicked off our shoes, put our feet up, sank back into our old sofa, and waited for God to reveal the great destiny He had planned for us.

No one called.

Friends scattered to various jobs. Summer dragged past, and we were politely asked to leave our college apartment. We weren't students anymore. We didn't have careers. We were in a horrible new world, "The time between."

We rented half of a duplex in a rough neighborhood, our main criteria being a month-by-month lease as cheap as possible. No sense being tied into a long commitment. God had big plans for us, and we'd be getting our call soon.

I focused on my work with the Christian theater in town. It brought in almost no income, but many dear friends. Ted and I started hosting weekly Bible studies for some of the actors who were searching for a deeper walk with God.

Ted decided to sell encyclopedias. Or try to.

Each week we called the college office. "Has a call come in? Has anyone requested to meet with us?"

The answer was always the same. "Nothing yet."

Months dragged past. On a chilly November day, I hosted a leaf-raking party for the neighborhood children. After a puppet show with Kermit playing the role of the Good Samaritan, and a shared box of gingersnaps, the kids scattered like bright maple leaves in the wind.

I trudged inside to make a pot of tea. Ted arrived soon, shoulders drooping from another unsuccessful day of extolling the benefits of leather-bound reference books. We sagged into the sofa, cradling mugs of tea and trying to pull comfort from their warmth.

"I don't get it. We both asked God what we should do with our lives—which college to attend. We followed where He led us. And it wasn't easy. How can He ignore us like this?" I blurted out the words, then ducked my chin, ashamed of my anger.

"I don't know," Ted said quietly. We had counted on things falling into place once we graduated. The reality of daily uncertainty filled us both with a sense of failure. Everyone else we knew was busy in the "real world."

"Well, I'm not sure I like God very much right now." The words slipped out through my clenched teeth.

Beneath my irritation was bewildered pain. *Had God decided He didn't want our service? That He couldn't use us?* I swung between tantrums of anger and feelings of rejection. Woven through all the emotions was a constant frustration at this seeming waste of time.

We had worked so hard to finish college and be available for God to use us. Each night I crawled into bed and reminded God of the church programs I wasn't organizing, the Sunday school teachers I wasn't training, and the great work for Him that I wasn't able to accomplish—since He hadn't done His part and guided us to a church.

At last, six months after graduation, we received a call. Friends helped us load a U-haul and brave a blizzard to drive across the state to the church where we would serve.

We threw ourselves into the work for which we had trained.

But I couldn't let go of my confusion about the months of waiting. *Lord, why all that empty time? Why all those months where we did nothing of value?* I laid the questions down like cards on a table, and turned them over and over. *Please help me understand. It was such a painful time.*

Without words, a stream of memories flowed into my thoughts: the neighborhood children who had never heard a Bible story until we staged puppet shows for them; the theater friends who sprawled on our living room floor and dug into their walk with Christ with new zeal; the visitation skills Ted developed as he went into homes to sell encyclopedias; the casual conversations about faith issues we both had in our various odd jobs during those months; the joy of watching God provide groceries in unexpected ways when we didn't know how to stretch a dollar any further; the hours of searching, prayer, and blind stumbling.

The time between had not been an empty time. In fact, viewing it from the distance of years, I believe God accomplished more ministry through our lives in those six months of "uselessness" than in the following six months of "official" church work.

And perhaps one of His most important projects was to reveal unlovely motives and expectations lurking in my own heart, and to teach me that He measures value very differently than I had.

In the decades since graduation, I've experienced many other "times between." Weeks of praying for a friend with cancer. Months of job searches. Years of struggle with weaknesses that never seemed to improve.

The "time between" hope and fulfillment, dream and result, or planting and harvesting still tries my patience. But I've learned. Any fragment of time God chooses to touch is full of grace and value. Even "the time between."

the story of
francis barton

(As told to Linda Henson)

I can do all things through Christ who strengthens me.

PHILIPPIANS 4:13 NKJV

My dad had been sick for days, and now the doctor was telling us he had pneumonia. He had to have complete bed rest and wouldn't be able to work for nearly a year. How could this happen right now? My brother had recently come down with typhoid fever; my older sister was frail and couldn't work outside the house. I had two younger sisters who still felt life was for dolls and tea parties, and I hoped they could stay that way for a few more years. My dear mother had been doing some strange things; today she probably would be diagnosed with Alzheimer's. So she would be no help with the farm. She did the best she could tending the garden and helped with my brother and father.

It was midsummer, and there was plowing to be done. The crops were in good shape but needed attention the rest of the summer. And then there was the harvest! How would the crops be brought in? Without the crops we wouldn't be able to make the payments on the farm or have seed for another year. Our lives depended on this crop.

My head spun, and my knees grew a little weak as I began to realize that at sixteen I alone had the responsibility of saving my family from ruin. We had a farm of one hundred sixty acres of rolling southern Indiana farmland; Dad and I had planted the fields with corn, soy beans, and wheat. Eight cows had to be milked morning and night; and four horses, two mules, pigs, and chickens had to be fed. I didn't know how, but I was determined with God's help, I could do it.

I was up at 4:30 in the morning to milk cows and feed all those animals, back in the house for breakfast. With eggs, bacon from the hogs we raised, potatoes, home-made bread with jelly my mother had made during the summer, that was my favorite meal. But there was no real time to sit and enjoy it all because I had to hitch up the mules or horses and make haste to the fields.

Day after day, from morning to night I was busy. There was no time for any frivolity. But one thing my mother firmly believed in was going to church. Her father had been a circuit-riding preacher through the back-roads of Southern Indiana and Illinois. She had learned early on that faith was important in life. And really, the Sunday service was the only break from my daily job, and the one thing that gave me strength for the next week, even though, on that day of rest I still had to take care of all the animals.

The crops were thriving, and I felt proud of what I had accomplished; but it was far from over. As I started hearing the katydids chirp, I knew that fall was coming. Harvest time was near, and so was school. I had to make a decision that I never dreamed I would face. No one in my family had ever graduated from high school, and I was determined to break that pattern. I had dreams. But, now my dreams seemed to be clouded by the fact that I was needed at home to tend the farm.

There was no choice but to drop out of school for the year and take care of family needs. Even though it seemed I might have to prolong my school years, I determined that somehow I would graduate. Though it seemed impossible, I made up my mind that I would graduate with my class.

When the time came, neighbors who had heard of our situation came to help harvest the crops. So many showed up to help. Teams of mules and horses tramped up and down the fields harvesting the bountiful treasure from the fields. Ladies came too and brought dishes full of wonderful food. At noon they'd mount several boards across saw horses for a table in the yard and cover it with their bright table cloths. Then they'd fill it with the scrumptious meals they had prepared. There was always a five-gallon container of sweet iced tea that tasted so good on those hot days. The dinner bell called all the men to come in from the field and eat together. I think those days are some of my best memories.

I still remember the smell of the straw hats that the men removed at the table, their white foreheads and red cheeks permanently marking them as hard workers. Dinner gave us a short time for socializing and finding the newest ideas for farming or hearing of new babies in the community. I don't know what I would have done without the help of those good and decent people.

Spring found me once again in the fields, plowing, harrowing, planting, cultivating. On and on it went, day in and day out, up at 4:30 and early to bed. Those mules and horses became my only friends for a few months. My dad became stronger and stronger and began to help me; what a relief. Could I possibly be seeing light at the end of the tunnel?

By the end of the summer Dad was ready to take back his place as head of the family. And I was so glad to give it up. Now, I needed to turn my attention to my education. I was a year behind all of my friends. When I went in to talk with the principal, I told him I wanted to make up the eleventh grade and finish the twelfth grade all in one year. He had a look that told me he didn't think I could do it but was willing to let me try.

I took eleventh and twelfth grade English, geometry and twelfth grade math, Latin, literature, and on and on. My days were full, and my nights were spent studying. When we studied Shakespeare, the rest of the class struggled, but to everyone's surprise, I could understand it. I made the highest marks in the class.

It was another year of nothing but work, but this time it wasn't behind a mule. I had to walk a mile to catch the school bus, then ride four miles into Tennyson High School. That mile walk seemed gruesome when winter came and deep snow covered the road I had to travel. We lived in a little area called Degonia Springs where rich people came in the summer for the waters of the spring. Electricity hadn't been run back into the farmland, so I sat at the table studying by kerosene lamp.

Finally, the hard year passed, and so did I! I couldn't believe it. I had made it. I was going to graduate with my class. My mother, father, brother, and sisters sat beaming as I walked on the platform and shook the hand of the superintendent of schools.

I knew that I couldn't take all the credit. The day I walked down the aisle to receive my diploma was the proudest day of my life. I did my part, but I knew God had given me the strength and wisdom to accomplish the task. He blessed my efforts that year; He continued to do so throughout my life.

teacher at last

EUGENE EDWARDS

(as told to Gloria Cassity Stargel)

Delight yourself in the LORD and he will

give you the desires of your heart.

PSALM 37:4 NIV

January 15, 1993. It was now, or never.

At my shop that wintry afternoon, I pulled on my black overcoat and stepped outside. With my hand on the doorknob, I paused. *Well, Atlas Plumbing Company, I've devoted thirty years of hard work growing into a skilled plumber and you into a successful business. And you've been good to me and my family. But now I must follow my heart.* I shut the door for the last time and hung on it a sign: GONE OUT OF BUSINESS.

Then, feeling about as daring as David when he went out to fight Goliath with only a slingshot, I climbed into my '91 Burgundy Explorer and at age fifty, turned all thoughts toward my life-long dream of being a schoolteacher. *Lord, you've brought me this far,* I pleaded, *please don't leave me now, or I'll fail for sure.*

The teacher who taught me the greatest life lessons never would have called himself a teacher. Mr. Roy was my mentor, my role model, way back before either term was popular. Mr. Roy talked with me, asked me questions, just like I was someone special instead of a scrawny little black kid.

I was about six when we found each other over in Mayfield, South Carolina, where I was born. There was a little family-run store in our neighborhood with the American flag waving right next to the Coca-Cola sign above the screen door. Mr. Roy and some other old-timers were usually there, next to the pot-bellied stove, playing a round of checkers and swapping yarns. I'd sidle up to the checkerboard, to "help out" Mr. Roy with his game.

And it was there, at Mr. Roy's elbow, that many of my values and certainly my life goals were born. Not that my parents didn't teach me things. They did. By example they taught me the value of hard work and the importance of having the Lord in your life. But as there were seventeen of us children at home, individual attention was hard to come by.

"Eugene," Mr. Roy said one day, "'whatta' you want to be when you grow up?"

"A teacher," I blurted out. Then added with a self-conscious swagger, "That's what I wanna be—a school teacher."

In a tone which left no room for doubt Mr. Roy responded, "Then be one!"

Mr. Roy could see the pitfalls ahead, however. "Eugene," he said, dead-serious as he wrapped one bony arm around my equally thin shoulders, "There will be times when folks will say; 'You can't do that.' Just remember to take that in stride. Then set out to prove them wrong."

His advice might have worked, too, except that during my junior year of high school, my mom passed away. I knew then that my going to college and becoming a teacher was out of the question. Dad needed me to help him care for the younger children. So I took up a trade instead—plumbing.

I recalled another of Mr. Roy's admonitions. "One more thing, Eugene," he'd said. "Whatever you become, whether you're a ditch-digger or a school teacher, you be the best you can be. That's all the good Lord asks of us."

By then, Mr. Roy's principles had become my own. I told myself: *If I can't be a teacher, I'll be the best plumber in the business.* And that's exactly what I tried to do for thirty years. I learned all I could about the trade. Practiced what I believed—do it right the first time, and you don't have to go back. Eventually I had my own business.

In the early years I even managed to take an off-campus college course from time to time, but abandoned that effort when my plumbing business became too demanding. All the while, though, buried deep in my heart, the dream of someday being a teacher pulsed on.

It was in 1971 that I was able to send my daughter to college, and she has been a teacher ever since, currently teaching third grade in the public school system. *Maybe her teaching will satisfy my longing,* my subconscious said. *I can live my dream through her.*

That day came, though, when my long-desired dream would no longer be denied. *Eugene,* I said to myself, *You've always wanted to teach. You love kids. You see the great need for adult role models. You've prayed about it. Why don't you get out there and see if you can cut it?* And that's when I closed my shop and set out to find the answer.

Four days later, I started work at Hendrix Drive Elementary School. Not as a teacher, mind you, but as custodian. I traded my wrenches and pipe fittings for brooms and paint brushes and a 40 percent reduction in pay. I figured the job would be a good way to get a feel for the school environment, to test the waters, so to speak, to see if I could even relate to the youngsters of today.

Right away, I hit it off with the students. Out in the hallways running the floor polisher, I'd throw them a big high five, and they responded with wide grins and a "five back-at-you." Soon they were calling me Mr. Edwards, and the principal even let me read to some of the lower grades.

Often I found a youngster propped up against the wall outside his classroom, having been banished there for misbehavior of one kind or another. "Whatza matter, son?" I'd ask him, truly concerned. After he had related his current infraction of rules and I had emphasized his need to comply, I'd go in and talk with his teacher, smoothing the way for reconciliation and his return to the classroom.

Surprisingly, I made a very fine mediator, maybe because I could put myself in the mindset of these youngsters. So many—like my young friend Johnny—came from broken homes, being raised by a single mom or by a grandmother. They were hungry for a positive male role model, someone who would show genuine interest in them, show them they were loved. They desperately needed a Mr. Roy in their lives. I wanted to be that one.

I had time to do a lot of thinking, and praying, while I polished those floors. *Why, I have a ministry right here as a custodian. I'm making a difference in these young lives, in being able to encourage them, challenge them. Maybe I don't need to put myself through the rigors of college courses in order to help students. Even Principal Soper called me "an excellent role model."*

But I heard God say to me, *Yes, Eugene, all that is true. Yet, just think how much more effectively you can minister when you combine your inherent skills with proper training.*

All the while, like a long-play recording, I could hear Mr. Roy saying, "Never settle for second best, Eugene. Whatever you become, you be the best you can be." One night I ventured to the family, "Looks like I'm gonna have to go to college after all."

"Eugene, it's your turn to get that degree you've always wanted," my wife Annette said, throwing her arms around me. "We'll all help you."

"Yeah, Dad," Michael and Monique added, giving me a thumbs-up. "Go for it!"

So I did. In the fall of '94, I signed up for night and weekend classes at the Norcross branch of Brenau University.

I plain had the jitters when I approached those first classes. *Will I be the oldest student there? Am I too old, too tired to learn those tough subjects?* Even months later—during the twenty-mile drive—often I asked myself, *Eugene, do you know what in the world you're doing?*

Working forty hours a week at the school, before long I found myself studying many nights until 1 or 2 A.M., only to get up at 5:30 in order to be at work by 6:30. Often, while cleaning those floors, I carried on a running dialogue with Jesus. *Lord, I'm bone weary. Remind me again that this is something You want me to do. 'Cause I tell you the truth, if it's just my wanting it, I'm about ready to quit.*

In answer, I believe God sent Johnny back to me. Johnny had graduated our school the year before; now he came by to visit and found me about to replace a fluorescent bulb in a hallway fixture. "Johnny, I am so glad to see you!" I said, while giving him a big bear hug. "How're you doing, son?"

"Fine, Sir," he responded, his good manners impressing me beyond measure. "Mr. Edwards," he went on, "I want to thank you for the time you spent with me here, and for caring about me. I never would have made it through sixth grade if it had not been for you."

"Johnny, I am so proud of you," I responded, giving him my undivided attention. "And you're going to finish high school, aren't you?"

"Yes, Sir," he said, his face breaking into a huge smile, "I'm even going to college, Mr. Edwards! Like you!"

I almost cried to think I had influenced him that much. I determined then and there to stick it out with my studies. Johnny was counting on me. As would other Johnny's yet to come.

Now it is early morning—May 3, 1997—a day that will go down in history. My history, certainly. It's pouring rain, but who cares? Today is graduation day!

I'm driving Monique's '96 White Mustang up I-85 north the fifty miles to Gainesville for rehearsal. The family will follow for the ceremony at 10:00. I glance at my hand on the steering wheel and admire the blue-stoned college class ring on this fifty-five-year-old plumber's work-worn finger. On the seat beside me is my black robe and mortarboard with tassel. Out loud I keep saying, "Praise you, Jesus! Thank you, Jesus."

The rain has eased up by the time I park at the Georgia Mountain Center where Brenau University's Commencements are being held, this one for Evening and Weekend College Undergraduates. I sit there several minutes, basking in the glow. I can't deny it. Tears of happiness threaten to run down my cheeks.

At the 10:00 ceremony, I am almost overcome with emotion. As the music swells, the processional begins with the university president and faculty in full academic regalia looking impressive indeed, along with trustees of the university and the guest speaker: The Honorable Edward E. Elson, United States Ambassador to the kingdom of Denmark.

All those dignitaries remain standing to honor us as we file in—350 candidates for degrees. When my turn comes, I somehow get up onto the stage to receive my diploma, but I never feel my feet touch the floor!

I float back to my seat, beaming like a lit-up Christmas tree, clutching the tangible evidence of a long-desired dream come true: a square of parchment with those all-important words, Bachelor of Science Degree in Elementary Education.

Yessiree, my inner self is thinking, *just goes to show you. If you dream long enough—and work hard enough—the good Lord will help make your dream come true.*

A teacher at last! Mr. Roy would be proud.

pride without pomp and circumstance

DARLA SATTERFIELD DAVIS

"Live as free men...live as Servants of God."

1 PETER 2:16 NIV

"Graduation" was held in the cafeteria of a local high school with less than 20 people in attendance including the graduating class. There were no caps and gowns, decorations, podiums, or special speakers. No "Pomp and Circumstance" what-so-ever. However, it was one of the most significant and memorable graduations I have ever attended.

As I stood before my American Government Class of five students, I could hardly believe we were at the end of our course and that they would all be taking their U.S. Citizenship Test the following day. Three of the graduates were brothers, hardworking construction workers from Mexico. The rest of the class was made up of a small but outspoken Guatemalan man, and a charming Swedish woman who had lived in the United States with her husband for more than twenty years.

There they were, all dressed up and beaming with pride. My supervisor began the event by recognizing contributions that had been made to the United States by other past immigrants and told a brief history of the United States as the "Great American Melting Pot."

When it was time to hand out the diplomas, the eldest of the three brothers shook my hand hard, and with tears in his eyes told me I would never know how happy I had made him. "I love this country Maestra (teacher), and I am going to be an American Citizen tomorrow…and I thank you with my heart" he said.

"Me too…all of us!" said the next brother in line. "My Mamma will be so proud of us. She always want her boys here, and she say 'GO! Go, to the United States for a better chance!' We did come here, and now we stay!"

I swallowed hard and hugged each one of them as I handed them the diplomas. My Swedish student had made a pillow that looked like an Early American Flag. She had all of the students sign the pillow and presented it to me in return for her diploma. "I have been wanting this for over twenty years." she said with misty eyes. "Thank you so much, you made the history of this great country come alive for me."

The truth is *they* made the history of this country come alive for *me*. They had shared their struggles of trying to get here. The trials of learning a new language and the humorous mistakes they had made. Their fresh views of what seemed to them as "The Promised Land" lifted my heart and reminded me once again why I was proud to be an American.

It is easy to become negligent in regards to views of our own country; we sometimes forget how great America really is and why. I knew these graduates would remind many of us about the greatness of this country even with its flaws and faults. I knew they would be part of the continuing purpose of our country, and that they had already begun to make it just a little better place to live.

Take a moment to look at your world and all the opportunities that await you. Perhaps God has blessed you with supportive parents, or maybe a mentor who has championed and encouraged you to press on and reach for your personal best.

Whatever your circumstance, it is important to approach life with a heart of gratitude. Remember to thank those who have believed in you and acknowledge God for his blessings and direction in your life.

to stacee
with love

JOAN CLAYTON

You have made me very happy.

PSALM 4:7 NCV

Ten years ago I retired from a job that gave me multiple blessings. How I have missed the children. Even today, the sight of a school bus brings back fond memories. My treasure chest is full and running over.

Stacee is one of those memories. She still blesses me today with the joy I saw in my classroom. She brought sunshine to the days when the sand blew, when I had bus duty, playground duty, teachers' meetings, and when I had a headache.

Stacee grasped learning, literally savoring each assignment. She listened attentively to instruction. Her adoring eyes never left mine as they followed me around the classroom. Many times I prayed: *Lord, help me be the kind of teacher Stacee thinks I am.*

Stacee indeed became my teacher. As a second grader, she determined to be happy in life and gave that gift of joy to everyone she met. She wrote me notes every day, and they are all in my "Treasure Book." But more than that, she wrote her notes on my heart. She taught me the real meaning of unconditional love. Who would think I could learn so much from a seven-year-old? She taught me that happiness comes from within, not external circumstances.

When I told my last class I was retiring, the children cried and said, "Teacher, you don't love us anymore." Stacee consoled the class with her optimistic upbeat attitude, "We can still go to see her. We can still write to her," and so they did, many times, but it was Stacee, her mom, and sister who blessed my husband and me with many visits. It was Stacee who determined to still bring joy to a retiring teacher who missed the children. Always thinking of someone else, Stacee's heart is the happiest because it beats for others.

A bond exists between teacher and student that can never be severed. Students leave footprints on a teacher's heart, and Stacee has permanently left her footprints on mine.

She is destined for greatness. She makes the great moments in her life and doesn't miss a single one.

If I could speak to all of the students I taught over the course of my career, I would want to bless and thank them. My thirty-one years of teaching is filled to running over with wonderful memories. I will miss each one of my students, but the best is yet to be, and "I press on toward the mark. God has sent me children…angels who have grown in the garden of my heart!"

Thank you Stacee, for this wonderful honor. To have had you as a second grader and now as a graduating senior who has chosen me for the teacher who made the greatest influence upon your life, my heart is filled with unspeakable love and gratitude.

You will forever remain in my thoughts and prayers. I will never forget you, and I will always love you!

from a distance

NANCY B. GIBBS

**You will show me the way of life, granting me the joy of
your presence and the pleasures of living with you forever.**

PSALM 16:11 NLT

"IDEAS
ARE THE
BEGINNING
OF ALL
ACHIEVE-
MENT."

—Bruce Lee

A couple years ago, I sat on one of the bleachers at the
university gymnasium and looked into the ocean of people sitting
center-stage in the gym. They were all dressed in black caps and
gowns. As I stared into the crowd, I saw her. Our youngest child,
Becky stood out in the crowd. Her blond hair made her easy to
spot. I watched her as she scanned the audience in search of her
family and friends.

I stood up and walked into the aisle and waved. The instant
that she saw me a big smile covered her face. It was one of the
proudest moments in my life. My husband, Roy, and I had
worked hard. With three children and eleven straight years of
having one of them in college, our funds were running low. I

thought about how many of those years the two of us had held down at least two jobs to make this day possible. At that moment as I watched her smiling face, I realized that our time and money had not been wasted. Becky was graduating from college. The future before her was bright.

As parents, there was a realization that we had done our job well. We had encouraged our children to be the best they could be. They all held degrees from the universities of their choice. Our twin sons had jobs they enjoyed, and one had even provided us with a precious granddaughter. How blessed we had been.

For a few minutes I sat there and stared at Becky. From a distance, I could see hope written all over her face. I saw joy in her eyes as she spied the crowd of people attending the graduation on her behalf.

I saw her promising future, and yet, at the same time, I recalled her vivid past. It seemed like just a few weeks earlier when Becky had graduated from kindergarten. We felt so proud because she could add and subtract. Then I remembered her advancing from middle school to high school and receiving numerous honors. Before long we sat in the football field at her high school graduation and watched another chapter of our lives come to a close. When she left home to attend college, bittersweet feelings of hope and loneliness filled my heart.

Now several years later, we had reached yet another milestone in our lives. We had finished the course that we had begun more than a decade earlier. As we celebrated with a graduation party for Becky the following day, I thought back over the years and played a video tape in my mind of my daughter from the day she was born to the day she graduated from college.

All of our children's futures were secure, and I realized that I had a part in making them the incredible adults they had become. It was now time to make my own dreams come true! Briefly, I considered going back to college to obtain a degree of my own. At the time, however, my writing career was flourishing, and I didn't want to put it on hold to finish college.

Since we had fewer financial responsibilities at the time, I was able to slow down my pace in the outside world and focus more on developing my writing career. The day Becky graduated; I also graduated into a lifestyle that can only be described as God's way.

Looking at Becky, from a distance, taking her first steps toward living her dreams, I imagined myself living my future dreams as an author. Numerous book signings, speaking engagements, and ministry activities filled my mind's eye.

Today, all the things I imagined from a distance for myself have come to pass. I rejoice in the fact that I was willing to look toward the future and open my heart to the opportunities that God had available for me.

I may never personally wear a cap and gown and graduate from college, but I know I am exactly where God would have me to be at this point in my life. And furthermore, I cannot ever imagine myself doing anything else but living for Him.

the unlikely scholarship

MICK THURBER

Delight yourself also in the Lord; and He shall give you the desires of your heart. Commit your way to the Lord; trust also in Him, and He shall bring it to pass.

PSALM 37:4-5 NKJV

"HOPE AGAINST HOPE, AND ASK TILL YE RECEIVE."

—James Montgomery

The moment I stepped onto the field, I could feel the butterflies going crazy inside. My heart was pounding. The most important game I was ever going to play was finally here.

This game was huge and meant a lot to me for several different reasons. I was a senior in high school, and this was the last day of softball I would ever play with my school team. As I stood in my position near third base, I drew a cross in the dirt with my foot, took a deep breath, and asked God to help me. I wanted so much to have a good game.

Just one more good game.

That October day was cool and cloudy. The autumn season was just beginning to show signs of change. I could sense the buzz of energy and smell excitement in the air as my team, the underdog, was about to play our first game in the state championship softball tournament.

The game alone was enough to make me rather nervous, but sitting in the bleachers, just a few feet from third base, were three college softball coaches who had come to watch me play.

I had met these coaches earlier in the year, and they talked with me about playing for their schools. It was college recruiting time, and there were several coaches at this tournament taking one last look at players they were considering before offering them a scholarship. But I wasn't prepared for all three coaches sitting together—watching me. They were close enough for me to hear them talking to each other.

During warm-up practice, thoughts of earlier days and events leading up to this game swirled around in my mind. For as long as I can remember, my teammates and I talked about someday playing college ball. Some of them dreamed to play for large, Division 1 universities, while others considered smaller schools. I was really interested in only one school—OBU—

Oklahoma Baptist University. I wasn't sure why. I just knew I wanted to go there.

The team I played for was ranked as one of the best teams in our state. One year we were even ranked seventh in the nation. I loved playing ball. We played an average of 120 games a year. I loved the weekend tournament trips. I loved our coaches who worked with us for years during countless days of practice. But I especially loved my teammates. We felt like one big family then and still do even though we've all gone our separate ways.

I remembered how my dad and I spent so much time on the road driving to far-off tournaments. We talked about all kinds of things, when I wasn't enjoying a good snooze. We talked about softball—what was going on with the team, how I was playing at the time, the weaker parts of my game that needed improvement, and how all these things related to my life spiritually.

We discussed what the Bible says regarding how to be a good friend and how to encourage my teammates, how to practice and play with 100 percent effort "with all my heart as unto the Lord," how to respect and follow the lead of my coaches, and how to play for God's glory. This began to make a difference in the way I approached everything in my life. I discovered God had a very distinct plan and purpose for me— even while playing softball!

Sometimes God would speak to my heart very clearly through a softball experience—like a particular time when my hitting was not going well at all. A good bat swing depends so much on a proper grip and use of one's hands. No matter how much I trained, I just couldn't seem to get the hang of it. One day, during this long and agonizing period of struggle, my dad read to me a verse, Psalm 144:1. "Praise be to the LORD my Rock, who trains my hands for war, and my fingers to battle."

This verse deeply touched me at that moment—when I truly needed God to help me. I sensed God was gently speaking to my heart that He would be with me as I trained and would help me become a better hitter. That verse has stuck with me ever since.

The summer before a softball player's senior year in high school is when they should be playing at their best. That's when college coaches start to heavily recruit. But it seemed I was playing at my worst. When the season ended at the national tournament, I was going through a major hitting slump and committing fielding errors I normally didn't make. It caused me to worry if those colleges who had been originally recruiting me, might now be losing interest. And the one school, really the only school I wanted to hear from, had not contacted me at all.

I had written the OBU coach a letter but heard nothing back. Summer ball was now over. It was beginning to seem hopeless. High school softball started immediately after the summer season ended. The unanswered college questions always pricked my thoughts, but I found encouragement in God to just keep trusting in Him no matter how things looked. He reminded me that He was in total control.

My senior softball season had taken a turn for the better, and things were actually going good. My hitting had improved, and all my stats were up. My team had just finished a mid-season tournament in late September, and as we were heading toward the bus ride home, I noticed an unfamiliar woman walking toward me. She introduced herself. It was the head softball coach from Oklahoma Baptist University.

I was thrilled and quietly overwhelmed by God's faithfulness. We talked for several minutes, and she told me she would be in contact with me. She encouraged me to have a good season and said she hoped to see me again at "state." We spoke a couple of more times after that, and our team eventually did earn a spot in the state championship tournament.

So, there I stood at third base, getting ready for the first pitch of the big game. I was simply amazed at how all this was working out.

The umpire yelled, "Play ball!" I focused on the game and got into position. It wasn't long before the first ball was hit to me, a routine grounder. It seemed I had fielded a million of these over the years. I caught the ball clean and threw to first base for the out. There was one slight problem. As soon as I let the ball go, I wished that I could bring it back.

The ball sailed over the first baseman's head and into right field. I couldn't believe it. This was not the time to make such a crucial mistake.

I took a deep breath and tried to shake it off the best I could. I prepared myself for the next batter. Again, a ground ball was hit to me, and again, I overthrew first base. The ball soared into right field. I could only imagine what those coaches were thinking.

Feeling the pressure and disappointment of two mistakes in a row, I readied myself again for the next batter. For a third time I scooped up a sharply hit ground ball, and for the third consecutive time I hurled the ball into deep right field. I could feel my shoulders slump as I sighed heavily. I stood there stunned, bewildered, and discouraged. My coach and teammates were perplexed. I just didn't make errors like this. *What was going on? Did I just choke in the biggest game of my life? Did I just throw my chance for a scholarship into right field?*

All I could think was, *God, I know you are still in control. I'm trying my best, and I know You love me. But I just don't understand why this is happening.*

The game didn't go much better for the rest of the team either. After seven grueling innings, we lost. Our team shook hands with the winners and packed our bags to leave the dugout. I can remember seeing those coaches stand up from the bleachers and walk slowly over to the next field...all except one...the coach from OBU.

She came over to me after our team meeting. She knew I was down and offered a warm, understanding smile, telling me to not worry about it. Things like this happen all the time. She encouraged me to keep playing hard and said she'd call me later.

Slowly the days passed by. No phone calls. No letters. Nothing.

Was OBU still a possibility? Did I completely fail? All I know is that for the next few days after the state tournament God was my rock. He gave me a peaceful heart. He gave me the assurance that He would take care of me.

At last, I received a phone call. It was the coach from Oklahoma Baptist University. She invited me to the school for an official recruiting visit and offered me a scholarship to play softball—which I gladly accepted. When my dad asked the coach what she thought when I threw the ball into right field three times, she told us that it actually made her very happy. She cheered to herself—under her breath—hoping the other coaches might become less interested. She wanted me at OBU.

My heart is grateful to the Lord for my unlikely scholarship. God showed me something very special that day, that even now during the darkest times, when I can't see the way, when everything seems hopeless—He is still there. Always faithful. He will never leave me and will always carry out His plans for me even when it doesn't seem to make sense.

the God of second chances

TEENA M. STEWART

Rid yourselves of all the offenses you have committed,

and get a new heart and a new spirit.

EZEKIEL 18:31

The photo of Gabby and her friends radiated an electrical charge of excitement. With wide-eyes and surprised faces they stood right next to actor Kevin Costner who looked very celebrity-ish and respectable in his designer shades. The Pebble Beach Golf tournament was a big deal to golfers, as well as celebrity followers. Looking at the photo, Gabby recalled how the whole Pebble Beach thing had felt like an out-of-body experience. She wasn't there as a paying part of the crowd. She and her friends were working the tournament catering to earn college credits for their culinary arts certificate, plus some extra pay.

The work required them to rise as early as 4:00 A.M. to chop, slice, dice, and simmer to prepare the day's delicacies. On that day, when their shift ended, she and several of her friends decided to explore the area, a privilege that came with working the tournament. Still dressed in their chef coats, the group of students wandered the golf course's surrounding tents and displays.

One of the girls grabbed Gabby by the arm when she spied a familiar face. "Is that...is that..." she whispered excitedly, but before she could say the actor's name, Kevin Costner spied them. Their white coats made them easy to spot, and whether it was their youth, the coats, or simply a God thing, the actor noticed them and motioned them over.

He chatted with them briefly and offered to take a picture by holding one of the girl's cameras at arm's length and snapping a picture of himself with them. A flock of press photographers saw it as a prime opportunity. Snap, snap, went the cameras. A day later their laughing images were captured for all to see in the newspaper along with Kevin Costner.

Just a few years earlier, before moving to California, Gabby visited Johnson and Wales, a respected culinary arts college in Denver. She had loved to cook for as long as she could remember, and becoming a chef was her life-long dream. There were so many different choices within the field. She could have been a pastry chef, a purchaser, a restaurant manager, or even a personal chef. But her hopes fell when she realized how hard it was to be accepted into such a prestigious college. When she looked at her older sister who was already in college, it made the situation seem even more bleak. *Why couldn't she be a good student like her sister?* Everybody was supposed to go to college after high school. At least, that was how it seemed.

Her mother had pleaded, threatened, and cajoled her to take her grades more seriously. But, in her junior year of high school, her grades hit an all time low. Just when things seemed like they couldn't get any worse, her parents broke the news that they were all going to have to move to a different state because her father was taking a new job. Suddenly all her mom's warnings and threats about not graduating because of poor grades became very real.

For the next couple of months it seemed she was locked into meetings. There was the one where her parents sat down with her to talk about the facts regarding changing schools and the credits she needed to graduate high school. She sobbed at the kitchen table. "I wish I had listened to you, Mom." She said, "You were right. You tried to tell me. Why didn't I work harder? I've really messed things up."

Her mom's voice was soothing. "Gabby I know now that you have been frustrated with school!" Gabby blew her nose as her mother continued. "The important thing now is just to concentrate on getting the credits you need to graduate high school. Don't think about college right now. You don't need that added pressure. Your dad made an appointment for us to meet with the high school counselor at the new school to talk about your options."

A few months later, following their move, she and her parents had another meeting, this time with the new school's guidance counselor. The counselor explained. "It's going to be tough. There's very little margin for error, but you can still graduate." The counselor mapped out a plan for taking the courses necessary for Gabby to get her high school diploma. Then she said something amazing, "Our area here has some really good community colleges. One of them has a great culinary arts program. Even with excellent grades, I would still recommend that you start by enrolling in a community college culinary arts program." She went on to explain why. "It gives you a foundation of core courses, and many of the culinary arts colleges won't accept you without experience."

Gabby's heart gave a little flutter. Hope had struck a chord in her heart. The move to the new state, the opportunity to make good on her grades, and the fact that she actually might be able to attend a college and learn culinary arts skills seemed too good to believe.

That evening she apologized again to her mother, "Mom, I'm sorry. I should have listened, but I didn't. You did everything you could to try to motivate me to take school more seriously." Her mom nodded her head sympathetically. "I know. I finally decided I had to let you find out for yourself."

Gabby then said a silent prayer to God, thanking Him for giving her so many second chances, and she promised to work hard and finish out her senior year. She did, much to everyone's delight, and that fall she started in the culinary arts program at a local community college. The next spring she had the opportunity to attend the Pebble Beach Golf Tournament.

Gabby studied the picture of Kevin Costner with her friends, which her parents had proudly mounted on the wall. The past year and a half had been packed full of learning experiences and, yes, some fun!

She couldn't believe how much she had learned about food service in such a short time, and yet there was still so much more to know. Lately she had been thinking about trying to get into Johnson and Wales. It would take her schooling to the next level. Catering for the Pebble Beach Golf Tournament would look fantastic on her resume and might even aid with her acceptance. Maybe she would check into applying in the near future. She still felt unsure sometimes, but knew God had always been there for her. And with God's help her dream could still come true. He was, after all, the God of second chances.

who signed Jesus up for calculus 101?

LAURIN MAKOHON

Whatever you do or say, let it be as a representative of the Lord Jesus, all the while giving thanks through him to God the Father.

COLOSSIANS 3:17 NLT

Through the lens of high school, my life looked picture-perfect. I had a near-perfect GPA and a long-time boyfriend. My college application was stacked with extracurricular activities and accomplishments. Honors classes. AP classes. Class Vice President. Two-sport MVP. All-county. All-state. All-American. I'd spent the first eighteen years of my life trying to prove I was valuable. I wanted people to notice my achievements so that maybe, just maybe, they'd notice *me*. But although I graduated high school with a stellar resume, and I knew a lot of things, I didn't know myself very well.

I kicked off college following the same thought process I had followed in high school. *Achieve. Get noticed. Become somebody.*

My academic ego took a nosedive however, when I royally bombed my very first calculus test. (Just for the record, I still hate calculus.) After our professor returned our papers, I sat at my desk mentally repeating, *I am in college, I am a big girl, I can't cry about this right now,* like a mantra. While the professor went over the answers, I was trying to remember how to breathe. I had gotten more questions wrong than right!

I tried to hide my sniffles by faking that I had a cold. Apparently my tears gave me away. Because after class, my brand-new friend of three weeks, David, asked if he could walk me back to my dorm room.

As we made our way back to the dorms, he strategically left out the fact that he had aced the test. (And I mean aced. It ends up that David never received anything other than A's in college. He was studying neurology.)

He offered to help me out. And he did. He spent the rest of the semester patiently teaching me the math concepts that I obviously didn't understand. And once in the middle of one of my mini-fits of Calculus-induced frustration, he explained that the God who made me may not have made me a math genius, but He didn't make a mistake.

Months after the Calculus fiasco, my boyfriend of four years decided to pursue his minor league baseball career and not me. I didn't go to class for a week. (I don't recommend this, by the way. It's pretty rough on your report card. And that didn't help matters much.) I rarely peeled myself out of my pajamas. (Don't try this either. Your roomies will get a little freaked out.) But another new friend, Christine, stopped by my apartment with a box of tissues and a pizza.

She listened while I whined about my shattered dreams. And my newfound hatred for all things related to baseball. And whether or not anyone would ever really love me and think I was beautiful. But after two hours of listening and full of pizza, she explained that God not only thought I was beautiful, He had made no mistakes in the way that He had put me together.

She explained that the God of the universe was not only pursing my heart, He was the lover of my soul. And she prayed for me. Out loud. Every time I had a breakup-induced breakdown in the weeks and months that followed, she would lovingly remind me that God was in the business of healing hearts. And she would pray for me.

It became obvious to me that I was missing something in my life. And I knew that God was in the Bible. So I found one, picked a page, and started reading. I had no clue what it said. I remember looking at it like it was hieroglyphics. The "thees" and "thous" really threw me for a loop. *Who talked like that in real life?* So the Bible found its way to my closet.

I did decide to go to an on-campus Fellowship of Christian Athletes meeting. There I met another new friend, named Natalie, who said the same things as Christine and David. She and I talked about life as a college athlete and explained that the athletic gear I proudly showed off on campus didn't determine who I was; my Creator did. She said that God had declared me valuable the moment He made me. And that my stats, my grades, my boyfriend (or lack of one), and my college application didn't affect how He felt about me one bit.

I wasn't quite convinced. So we decided to meet for lunch to talk some more. A couple of days later in a restaurant near campus, she shared a little booklet about Jesus with me. I took it home, pulled out my Bible, and tucked it inside.

The booklet sat there for a couple of weeks. And, every once in a while, I thought about what it said. The statement "God loves you" seemed so trite. So cheesy. So churchy. But the more I thought about the booklet, the more it seemed that God had to care about my life, and had a plan for my life.

Apparently this booklet wasn't my first run-in with Jesus. I had met Him before. He had just gone by different names. First, as David. Then as Christine. Then as Natalie. So I talked to Him about getting involved in my life. And He did.

Over the next few years, and through many more trials, I have learned that Jesus has a few more names. He also goes by Katie, Peyton, Ryan, Michelle, Luke, Jessie, Sam, Dan, Shannon, Wynn, and many others.

I have also learned that God has entrusted those who know Him with the most important accomplishment of all—representing Him. And because of their example, and because of the God that they love, I now do too, and I'm in the process of proclaiming His name as loud as I can.

letting go

TONNA CANFIELD

**I prayed for this child, and the LORD has granted me
what I asked of him. So now I give him to the LORD.
For his whole life he will be given over to the LORD.**

1 SAMUEL 1:27-28 NIV

I looked down at this precious little life snuggled in my arms
and understood what it meant to love, truly love unconditionally,
unselfishly, and completely.

During the months that I carried her, I prayed for God to help
me to know how to take care of her. I prayed that she would
come to know Christ at an early age. I prayed for her health, and
the list goes on and on. Now, here I was looking at this
incredible person who would change my life in so many amazing
and wonderful ways.

The time passed so quickly. She was no longer an infant but
an active toddler attending tea parties and Barbie dolls filled our

"YESTERDAY
IS GONE.
TOMORROW
IS YET TO
COME. WE
HAVE ONLY
TODAY. IF WE
HELP OUR
CHILDREN
TO BE WHAT
THEY SHOULD
BE TODAY,
THEY WILL
HAVE THE
NECESSARY
COURAGE
TO FACE LIFE
WITH
GREATER
LOVE."

—Mother Teresa

days. Walks around the neighborhood and hours of reading storybooks filled our evenings. I can remember lying awake at night, dreading Natalie's first day of kindergarten, my mind full of questions, thoughts, and fears. *How can I take her to a strange place and leave her there with strangers to take care of her? Who will protect her? What if someone is mean to her? What if she gets hurt or sick? What if she gets afraid? What if she needs me?*

Now she's a senior in high school, and we've just ordered graduation announcements. I find myself lying awake in bed with all the same thoughts about her leaving the safety of home for college life. Letting go hasn't gotten much easier.

I can remember praying when I took her to kindergarten, *Lord, I have to turn her over to you. I have to trust you to take care of her when I'm not around.* But through the years I've realized that it has been Him taking care of her all along, even when I've been near.

Who was with her when I walked her to kindergarten for the first time and had to turn and walk away, leaving her with strangers? Jesus. Who healed her body when she was sick? Jesus. Who was sitting unseen in the passenger seat beside her when she took her car for a drive by herself for the first time? Jesus. Who comforted her when her best friend betrayed her?

Jesus. Who mended her heart the first time a thoughtless boy broke it? Jesus. It may have been my shoulder she cried on, but it was His Spirit that comforted her.

I have to remind myself that it has been Jesus looking out for her all along, always working things for her good. I must remember that she was His before she was ever mine. Jesus will be with her, just as He always has, as she begins this new and exciting journey into college and adulthood.

life goes on

NANCY B. GIBBS

Man's goings are of the LORD; how can a man

then understand his own way?

PROVERBS 20:24

The day my daughter, Becky, graduated from high school was a bittersweet day. She enjoyed her junior and senior year and wasn't overjoyed at the idea of being handed a diploma and offering her friends a sad farewell.

"Why can't things stay the same?" she asked me earlier that day.

"Life goes on," I explained. "You will go to college, find new friends, and start a new life. During our journey here on earth, God shows us different roads to take and gives us new bridges to cross."

As soon as the words left my mouth, the inevitable hit me like a ton of bricks. My baby would soon be spreading her wings and leaving home. I wiped away tears, as I watched her march out on the field, dressed in her cap and gown, to receive her diploma. I decided that she wasn't the only one changing direction in life. As a parent, what would I do with the rest of my life?

Sure enough, the summer sped by, and Becky enrolled in college. I couldn't believe how quiet the house had become. It seemed the only time the telephone rang was when a telemarketer had an offer.

One lonely day I curled up on the sofa and cried. I missed my three children terribly. What would I do now that they had left home?

A few weeks passed, and our twin sons, Brad and Chad, came home for a visit. "You've always wanted to write Mama. Why don't you give it a try?" Chad asked.

"It's funny you would mention that," I explained. I felt led to write just a few nights ago. "But at forty-two years old, I sometimes feel that I missed my opportunity," I told him. "The odds seem so slim of ever being published when a person is young, and just the thought of me becoming successful at my age makes me laugh."

"Well, the Internet can help you get started, Mama," he explained. "I think you ought to give it a try."

I signed online and was instantly fixated with it. I found dozens of places to submit my writings, enter contests, and receive constructive feedback from others. Before long that lonely feeling was transformed into something positive. I couldn't wait to get up in the mornings to read some of the responses to my stories. Upon winning an honorable mention in the first writing contest I entered, I was elated.

With renewed motivation, I contacted my local newspaper and began writing a weekly column. I then gathered up the courage to submit stories to various publishing companies, magazines, and other periodicals. Even though I received my share of rejections, along the way, I learned some valuable lessons from the feedback I received.

I soon discovered that if I focused only on the rejections, it seemed that writing wasn't worth the effort. When I changed my thought patterns, however, I came to the conclusion that writing was much more than being published. I felt a sense of encouragement. Once I decided that I would write regardless of whether or not I ever received a big break, positive things began to happen.

My husband and I have become closer in recent years, and my writing accomplishments have multiplied. I think back to the day my daughter was graduating and to wiping away those tears. I realized that feeling sorry for myself would get me nowhere. I could have chosen to forget my dreams and settle for second best. But instead, I had a realization that as long as we have breath, we are free to dream. I set a tough goal for myself and reached it with a great deal of hard work. Like I explained to Becky that spring day, life goes on, and things must change.

It has been several years since Becky walked across that stage and received her high school diploma. While I continue to miss my children greatly, I have discovered that a wonderful life is here for me as long as I strive to be the best I can be. We are never too old to make our dreams come true. And when we change the course we are taking in life and head in the direction God wants us to go, amazing things can and do happen.

hiring God for the job

JANET LYNN MITCHELL

But I said to you, "Don't be afraid! The LORD your God is going before you. He will fight for you, just as you saw him do in Egypt. And you saw how the LORD your God cared for you again and again here in the wilderness, just as a father cares for his child. Now he has brought you to this place."

DEUTERONOMY 1:29-31 NLT

During my junior year of high school, I found myself entering the hospital preparing for surgery. Months earlier I had torn the cartilage in my knee and needed to have it removed. About 8:00 P.M., Dr. Allgood came into my room.

"Hey, Kiddo, are you ready for the morning?"

"Ready as I'll ever be," I responded.

"Why don't you hop up on your bed and let me take a last look at that knee of yours."

Dr. Allgood pulled the curtain around my bed. I sat on top of my sheets, as he slid my gown up over my knees, resting it on my thighs. He took my right leg in his hands and began to maneuver it in different directions, seeing if it would catch or lock. Laying it down, Dr. Allgood then took my left leg and performed the same exercise. I saw a glimpse of surprise in his facial expression as he laid my left leg back down.

Puzzled, he walked to the foot of my bed and grabbed my feet. He held them together, pointing my toes to the ceiling. Then, keeping my heels together, he slowly turned my feet outwards, keeping an eye on my knees. Grabbing the pen out of his pocket, he wrote numbers and measurements directly on the sheets.

What's he doing? I wondered.

Before I knew it, my gown was gathered around my waist, and my hips were being examined. I was turned to my right side and flipped to my left. First, my legs were in the air; then I was face down, looking straight into the bed.

What in the world is he doing? I thought.

"Janet, it seems that you have a congenital deformity."

"A what?" I said still face down, talking into the pillow.

"Your knees and your feet don't line up."

"They don't what?" I asked, while turning myself over so I could see the doctor.

"It's a rotation problem."

"It's a problem? I've got a problem?" *Oh, God, help me!*

Within minutes, Dr. Allgood left my room and gathered every doctor and resident he could find. Several people then crowded around my bedside. Again, I performed acrobatic tricks while Dr. Allgood explained his diagnosis to his colleagues. "Janet has excessive retroversion of her femur with external rotation of the tibias."

"What? I have what?"

"Anything surgical I'd suggest would be done at the tibial level, cutting and derotating the bones."

"What? Surgery? Oh, but Dr. Allgood," I interrupted. "I don't need surgery. I'm getting along fine."

Regardless of what I thought, Dr. Allgood continued. "Janet, I'd like you to walk down the hall to the nurses' station and back. We'd like to see your gait—how you walk. Hold your gown up over your knees so we can get a good look."

A good look? How embarrassing! I shut my eyes for a moment wishing I could make myself disappear.

"Janet, we're waiting," he repeated. "Will you walk?"

Hesitantly I slid out of the bed and slowly gathered my gown in my fingers. "Higher, higher, Janet, you've got to pull it way up."

Without facial expression, I began to walk the corridor. Nurses stood in their tracks and watched the procession of doctors following me as I paraded down the hall.

Is my gown high enough, I feel it's too high! I could feel the tears welling up inside of me. *God, help me. You said that I was perfectly and wonderfully made! Truthfully, right now I feel like the new freak at the circus!*

Soon, I made my way back to my room and sat down on the side of my bed. "Janet, we're concerned about your future."

"My future! How does this affect my future?" I asked as I burst into tears.

"Janet, we're worried that severe crippling arthritis will develop in your knee joints. The likelihood of you becoming wheelchair bound is great without surgical intervention."

Wheelchair bound? Arthritic changes?

I had gone from a "happy-go-lucky teenager" to one with an unbelievable worry in a matter of moments. Yet, even with Dr.

Allgood's "new discovery" my morning surgery went as planned. Weeks soon passed. I was able to walk without the help of my crutches, but my life seemed to evolve around second, third, and fourth opinions regarding my congenital deformity.

Throughout the next few months, I found it difficult to get my mind off the words "cripple" and "wheelchair." With Dr. Allgood's encouragement, I signed up to go to winter camp— skiing with the youth group from my church.

The snow at Badger Pass was like cotton under my skis. From the top of the slope, I scanned the scenic view and realized that my worries had traveled with me. *I can't imagine being crippled and never walking again!*

I took a deep breath, and in the middle of giving myself a pep talk, my thoughts began to shout. *Janet, you can do this. You've got to do this! If having surgery is what I need, I'll have it! I'll do whatever I can to—to prevent...*

Then with mounted determination, I pushed off and skied down the mountainside, completing a perfect run.

Despite my determination to face my problems head on, once at the bottom of the run I found myself worrying again. Throughout the remainder of the day, I caught myself daydreaming about my upcoming doctor appointments.

That night as I lay in bed I hid my face deep in my pillow as the concerns of my future overwhelmed me. I had done my best to convince my friends that I was fine, and my upcoming surgeries were simply a matter of fact. Yet, I was scared, fearful of both the known and unknown.

The following night at camp I sat and listened to the speaker. "Don't you think God is big enough to take care of your worries?" he asked. "Do you know how good it feels to let go—to let God do your worrying for you as you fall back into God's arms and experience Him catching you?"

Immediately I began to cry. I could feel my heart pounding as I yelled through my thoughts, *No, No, I don't know!* I hid my face trying not to be conspicuous as I fought with my emotions. Unable to control them, I snuck out of the meeting and headed straight to an old rustic prayer chapel hidden at the end of a trail. Making sure I was alone I slipped through the door and stumbled as I knelt below the stained glass window.

God, I'm so scared. I'm just sixteen, and these worries are too big for me. I need Your help! I need Your strength! I want You to do all the worrying that needs to be done. I guess my job is just to trust that You will.

Tears of release streamed from my eyes. In those few moments I told God that I resigned from worrying and hired Him for the job. It felt good to fall back into God's arms and then, with expectation, I would watch and experience God as He tended to my every need.

when you've done all to stand, stand!

TONNA CANFIELD

Be strong with the Lord's mighty power.

Put on all of God's armor so that you will be able to

stand firm against all strategies and tricks of the Devil.

EPHESIANS 6:10-11 NLT

"She has remained faithful to God since she was four years old! Why is He doing this to her?" My teenage daughter had accepted Christ at a very young age, only four years old. She had grown in her faith and had an unusual understanding of God's character that was far beyond her years. The past several months had been difficult for her. Always such a polite, shy, and good natured child, I had watched through the years as some took advantage of her kindness.

Her heart was recently broken by the betrayal of her best friend. The unkind words and callous silences of some girls at our church only added to her pain. The other girls seemed to think she was getting too much attention for her success in Bible quizzing and too many compliments on what a beautiful girl she had become. My daughter, being shy, was embarrassed by all the compliments and attention she was getting; she just wanted to have friends at church.

One day after she hung up the phone and began sobbing, as she was faced with more unkind comments made by girls she so desperately wanted as friends, the stress of watching her suffer needlessly became too much for me to silently bear. Her Bible quizzing coach had just called and told her that the other girls on her team didn't want her to be the captain anymore. She expressed her own distress and said she felt this was prompted by jealousy and that she would deal with it. My daughter liked these girls and was simply crushed.

I boiled with anger, angry with the girls that were making my daughter miserable, angry with the coach for telling my daughter what the other girls had said, angry that my daughter had always shown kindness to these girls and this was how she was being repaid, and angry at God for knowing all about it and not stopping it! That is when the words tumbled out of my mouth.

"She has remained faithful to God since she was four years old! Why is He doing this to her?"

Immediately, my daughter arose from her chair and looked me square in the eye, and more firmly than I have ever heard her speak, she said, "I will not sit here and listen to you blame God! God is not the one doing this to me! People are. God is the one helping me through it!" She silently walked to her room and quietly closed the door.

I felt smaller than I've ever felt in my life. The guilt overwhelmed me because I knew my daughter had spoken the truth. I was blaming God for something He didn't do, instead of thanking Him for the life lesson He was teaching my child.

I walked slowly to her room and opened the door. She was sitting on her bed crying. I sat down beside her and put my arms around her. I told her how proud I was of her and how thankful I was for her faith in God. I also told her that she was right, and that I knew God would be her strength. We prayed together, and I asked God to forgive me and to comfort us both.

Four years have passed since that day. God, of course, has been faithful to take care of my daughter. No, that wasn't the last time she has had to suffer unjustly. But God keeps working things out for her good and His glory. He keeps teaching us both important spiritual lessons. I am amazed at His patience with me.

My daughter has won many awards and honors that have made me so proud, but I have never been more proud of my daughter than the day she stood up for God, even if it meant standing up to me. I realized that she had a true understanding of what it means to love God above everyone else. No matter what anyone ever does to her, they can't take that away from her.

I have never forgotten the lesson I learned from my daughter that day. It is burned in my memory and in my heart. I want to stand up for God, even if it means standing alone.

mispronunciations

ANNETTEE BUDZBAN

Ye are blessed of the Lord which made heaven and earth.

PSALM 115:15

As a young girl, I wondered why my parents decided to spell my name in an unusual manner. My mother told me it was a French spelling. To me, it only spelled trouble. My name is Annettee, pronounced "Annett." The e's at the end are silent. The typical spelling is Annette with one e at the end, but mine was different—it included two e's at the end.

I felt frustrated because people always left off the second e, or they told me my name was misspelled. I longed for a more commonly spelled name like Carol or Amy. But this was the name I was given.

More than twenty years ago, when I was in nursing school, a good friend of mine started calling me "Annet-tee—her emphasis was put on the e's at the end. Now people were not only spelling my name incorrectly but pronouncing it incorrectly, as well. As our graduation day was approaching, she started to tease me that they would announce me as Annet-tee just as she did. I would cringe inside each time this was even suggested.

Finally, graduation day was here. It was a day filled with excitement and activity. In the morning a pinning ceremony for the nurses had been scheduled, and in the afternoon, there would be festivities which included the entire graduating class for the college.

The pinning ceremony was very meaningful. It was our first opportunity to dress as an official nurse—no more student nurse uniforms. We were called to the stage dressed like angels of mercy, in white from head to toe—from our white shoes to our nursing caps.

As they called each of our names, we received our nursing pins. To my relief, my name was pronounced correctly. The day would go without a glitch, or so I thought. The graduation ceremony was still ahead.

As I entered the auditorium for our graduation, it was filled with a sea of blue caps and gowns, and unfamiliar faces. We sat in alphabetical order until it was our turn to approach the stage. The moment had arrived. My name was next on the list. I heard the call—"Annet-tee Ford." I couldn't believe my ears. My friend cursed me with that name. I knew she was sitting in her seat roaring with laughter when they called me by her pet name. But I walked on that stage with pride. At that moment I made a choice. I was not going to let this spoil my day or my life, ANYMORE. Instead, I chose to see the beauty in my name. I would no longer be embarrassed by its mispronunciations or misspellings.

What happened that day was more than a graduation from nursing school and college. I graduated to see that with this unusual name, I had truly been blessed and not cursed.

dairy queen
rescue

MARTHA CURRINGTON

And it shall come to pass, that before they call, I will answer;

and while they are yet speaking, I will hear.

ISAIAH 65:24

It had started as a routine, hum-drum evening shift. I worked as a cashier at the downtown Dairy Queen in the rural town of Jasper, population, approximately 14,000. It was pay day. Everyone, including me, had already cashed the check. We all had cash in our purses. It was the only week night that a male wasn't there when we closed. Instead, Mrs. King, an older woman and the store owner, was with us.

The business closed exactly at eleven o'clock. We grabbed our purses and headed for the back exit together, for protection. I carried the last small bag of garbage out with me—my purse strapped over my shoulder. A soft drink in a paper cup was in my left hand.

As Mrs. King was locking the back door, the other two teenage girls we worked with stayed near her; everyone was facing the door with their backs toward me. I had stepped to the left to put the garbage into the bin. Just as I turned back around, I saw them! Two pair of legs, dressed in denim jeans, were visible beneath the drive-thru sign. Just as I opened my mouth to warn the others, two slim males darted out, one from each end. The silver barrels of their guns glistened in the moonlight.

"Get back inside! Get back inside!" one shouted frantically. Mrs. King unlocked the door, and we were all forced back inside the dimly lit building.

Once we were in the hallway, the one who had spoken nervously shouted, "Drop your purses to the floor!" Several thuds sounded as they hit the tile covered concrete. "You three, get inside the stockroom, hands on your heads!" The one who had not yet spoken held his gun pointed at us and stepped back into the stockroom with us, leaving the door partially open.

With the soft drink still in my left hand, resting on top of my head, I nervously glanced upward, trying to identify the gunmen. Both appeared to have very dark complexions. But I could see the one with us had rubbed some type of black substance all over his arms. Daring to glance slightly upward again, I could see he had done the same to his face. He was wearing a ball cap so I couldn't make out his hair type or color. It suddenly dawned on me, "That's why he's not talking. He's in disguise!"

Finally, I cautiously glanced out the open door and down the hallway. The other man had the end of his pistol barrel pressed against Mrs. King's forehead! He was shuffling back and forth, barrel still against her forehead. "Show me the safe, or I'll blow your...head off!" She, with her purse still over her shoulder, and with unusual calmness replied, "We don't have a safe."

She had refused to drop her purse when we dropped ours. She was still holding onto it tightly. I figured the deposit money was inside. He screamed it again and again at her, and she always gave the same calm reply. So he yelled aggressively, "Then hand over the night money!" Still answering calmly, she said, "All the money has already been sent to the night depository." I thought she was going to get us all killed for sure!

During all this time, I had been silently praying, more like pleading, *"Please God, send us some help! Please, please, God! Nobody knows that we're still here but you!"* Constantly I prayed!

It seemed like forever we stood there in the stockroom with a gun pointed at us. The other two girls were softly crying, and their bodies were trembling. Being a middle aged woman, I did my best to appear calm, hoping it would comfort them in some way.

Then, unexpectedly, the back door buzzer rang! What sweet music to my ears! The would-be robbers panicked and rushed for the door, with Mrs. King running right behind them!

The men shoved the door open fiercely, almost knocking someone down. We thought it was a policeman, but it was Carol, another teenage employee. Her car keys went flying from her hand. Mrs. King jerked her inside by the arm, as she slammed the door shut! We all knew that it couldn't be opened from the outside without a key! When we took garbage out or went out to clean the parking lot, we had to ring the buzzer so someone inside could open the door for us.

"Stay away from the windows! They might try to shoot their way back in!" Mrs. King shouted. Then she ran into the office and phoned the police department. The policemen arrived in a matter of minutes, but the men had gotten away.

Carol had worked with us but had clocked out early. She had kept her car keys in her pocket, so she was half way home before she realized she had forgotten her purse. She returned, hoping to still find us here. Coincidence? You'll never convince me that it was!

After being questioned about descriptions, and refilling my drink several times, the policemen allowed me to go home. I was still shaken while driving the fifteen miles home, alone, on a sparsely traveled country road, but when I arrived in my own front yard I finally began to calm down.

God had answered my pleading prayer during this crisis in a way I never could have imagined, just as He faithfully answers my prayers for everyday basic needs. I will never underestimate the power of prayer again, no matter what I face.

As I opened the front door and walked into my living room I realized something else. I was still holding my soggy, paper cup!

He had other plans for me than for my life to end that night. I have since become a writer. But occasionally, if I seem to be faltering, He reminds me of His great love and protection by recalling the Dairy Queen rescue to my mind. It never fails to work, and I breathe, *"Thank you, Lord. I understand."*

God has plans for your life as well. At times when you feel that you've lost your direction…look to Him. He'll always be there to help you back on the path He has planned for you.

*Names changed for privacy

living life God's Way

After reading these true stories of people who experienced God's grace and power in their lives, perhaps you realize that you are at a point in your own life where you need special help from God.

Are you facing a temptation? A broken relationship? A major disappointment?

Are you ready to experience forgiveness and salvation? Encouragement and hope? Wisdom and inspiration? A miracle?

Though God's power and grace are deep and profound, receiving His help is as simple as ABC.

A—Ask: The only place to start is by asking God for help;

B—Believe: You must believe—have faith—that God can help you;

C—Confess: You must confess—admit—that you truly need God's help to receive it.

Living life God's way doesn't mean that all troubles disappear, but it does mean that there will always be Someone to turn to with all your needs. Call on Him now. For more information on how you can live God's way, visit our website at:

www.godswaybooks.com

rights and permissions

meet the contributors

Candy Arrington is a freelance author whose publishing credits include *Writer's Digest, Discipleship Journal, Christian Home & School, The Upper Room, Focus on the Family,* and *Spirit-Led Writer.* She is a contributor to *Stories for the Teen's Heart, Vol. 3* and *Stories from a Soldier's Heart* (Multnomah). She coauthored *AFTERSHOCK: Help, Hope, and Healing in the Wake of Suicide* (Broadman & Holman Publishers, 2003). Candy lives in Spartanburg, South Carolina, with her husband, Jim, and their two teenage children, including Neely, who told this story.

Esther M. Bailey is a freelance writer with more than eight hundred published credits. She is coauthor of two books: *Designed for Excellence* and *When Roosters Crow.* She resides in Phoenix, Arizona, with her husband, Ray. You can e-mail her at baileywick@juno.com.

Lanita Bradley Boyd, a former teacher, is now a freelance writer who lives in Fort Thomas, Kentucky. In her writing she draws on her rural childhood, her many years of teaching, her work with churches in a wide variety of ministries, as well as family events and personalities.

Annettee Budzban is an author, freelance writer, and religion columnist. She has been published Worldwide on many e-zines and in magazines such as Guideposts Angels on Earth. Her e-mail address is ahrtwrites2u@aol.com

Tonna Canfield is a wife, mother, teacher, speaker, and author. She and her husband, Jeff, have been married twenty-one years. They have two daughters, Natalie and Erica. Tonna has been published in *Chicken Soup for the Mother* and *Daughter's Soul* and is currently writing a ladies' devotional book as well as a book about her own battle with depression. She may be reached at tonnacanfield@att.net.

Joan Clayton's newest release is a daily devotional. Joan is the religion columnist for her local newspaper. She has been included three times in *Who's Who Among America's Teachers.* She and her husband, Emmitt, reside in New Mexico.

Martha Currington, freelance writer and poet, lives in rural Alabama with her husband, Tom. She enjoys feeding, and admiring the great variety of wild birds in the area. She has poetry published in eleven anthologies. Other publishing credits include: Faith Writers Speak, Good Old Days Special(July,2003 issue), Purpose- a Christian pamphlet, The Daily Mountain, which also featured her as a front page "top story", and The Best of FaithWriters.com-Spring Edition

Darla Satterfield Davis is a native Californian residing in North Texas. She graduated with a B.S. degree in Education, minor in English. She has taught in public school for over 15 years and currently serves as art specialist for an elementary and intermediate school. Ms. Davis is also the Owner/Steward of *The Christian Fine Arts Center* in Cleburne, TX. where she teaches art, supervises the other fine arts classes, and manages the music venues and coffeehouse. She is available for speaking engagements during the summer months and can be contacted at: www.Christianfineartscenter.com.

Max Davis draws his insight from a vast and varied background—he has been a collegiate athlete, a truck driver, a coach, a pastor/counselor, and a vacuum cleaner salesman. Max holds degrees in journalism and lives with his wife, Allana, and three children on a farm outside of Baton Rouge, Louisiana.

Nancy B. Gibbs, the author of four books, is a weekly religion columnist for two newspapers, a writer for TWINS Magazine, and a contributor to numerous books and magazines. Her stories and articles have appeared in seven *Chicken Soup for the Soul* books, *Guideposts* books, *Chocolate for Women, Women's World, Family Circle, Decision, Angels on Earth, On Mission Magazine, Happiness,* and many others. Nancy is a pastor's wife, a mother, and a grandmother. She may be reached at daiseydood@aol.com or by writing P.O. Box 53, Cordele, Georgia 31010.

Linda Henson writes for a local newspaper and has contributed to various anthologies. She is a musician, counselor, and has taught language arts in the public school systems.

Sharon Hinck is developing a series of adventure fantasy novels that give encourgement to fight the daily battles of life. You may contact her at: writer@mn.it.com.

Jessica Inman is a newbie freelancer who writes essays and the occasional poem or short story; you can check out some of her work on

Boundless webzine (www.boundless.org) and TheOoze.com. She mourned the loss of Five Iron Frenzy, loves F.F. Bruce and Philip Yancey, and fancies herself an independent music buff.

Jennifer Johnson lives in Lawrenceburg, Kentucky with her husband and three daughters. To write about Abba is her passion. Jennifer plans to teach middle school after completing college.

Laurin Makohon is the assistant editor of *YouthWalk* magazine, a monthly devotional magazine for teens published by Walk Thru the Bible Ministries. She is a graduate of the University of Georgia and lives in Marietta, Georgia. She is addicted to Mexican food, Major League Baseball, and conversations with her friends over coffee.

Karen Majoris-Garrison is an award-winning author, whose stories appear in *Woman's World, Chicken Soup for the Soul,* and *God Allows U-Turns.* A wife and mother of two young children, Karen describes her family life as "Heaven on Earth." You may reach her at: innheaven@aol.com.

Janet Lynn Mitchell is a wife and mother of three. She is also an inspirational speaker and author of numerous articles and stories in compilations. Janet can be reached at Janetlm@prodigy.net or faxed (714) 633-6309

Amanda Pilgrim, Managing Editor for White Stone Books, resides in Tulsa, Oklahoma, with her husband, Mike, and their many animals. She is a former teacher and coach and enjoys writing about her experiences as an educator. She has been published in *Make Your Day Count for Teachers* and can be contacted at gsupreme@cox.net.

Michael T. Powers resides in Wisconsin with his wife Kristi. His stories appear in eighteen inspirational books, and he is the author of the book *Heart Touchers "A Celebration of Life."* For a sneak peek or to join the thousands of readers on his inspirational e-mail list, visit: ttp://www.HeartTouchers.com. You can e-mail him at: HeartTouchers@aol.com.

Gloria Cassity Stargel is an assignment writer for *Guideposts* Magazine; a freelance writer; and author of *The Healing, One Family's Victorious Struggle with Cancer,* published originally by Tyndale House Publishers. *The Healing* has been re-released in special updated edition by Bright Morning Publications. Call 1-800-888-9529 or Visit www.brightmorning.com.

Teena M. Stewart has worked in writing and editing for organizational newsletters and is a consultant/speaker with MinistryinMotion.net, a group that trains and equips leaders and volunteers to use their spiritual gifts and abilities for Christian ministry. She presently serves Northgate Christian Fellowship in Benicia, California, by teaching spiritual gifts/ministry discovery seminars and directing volunteer placement and equipping processes. You can contact Teena at teenastewart@teenastewart.com.

Cindy Thomson After twenty years of teaching, Cindy Thomson is using her gift of writing full time. She is a regular contributor to Family History Magazine and the Society for American Baseball Research publications. Her work has appeared in other compilations and she is a past winner in the Amy Foundation's Roaring Lamb awards.

Nanette Thorsen-Snipes is a freelnce writer of 20 years and an award-winning author. She began writing in 1981 when her mother was terminally ill with cancer. She began with a year of humorous family columns in a local newspaper. She always had an interest in writing—a strong desire was born at that time to write from her heart.

John "Mick" Thurber is a commercial designer and advertising specialist. He has been involved in the design of projects like the best-selling *Jesus Freaks* books, and is the creator of the *God's Way Series.* He lives in Bixby, Oklahoma, with his wife and three daughters.

tell us your story

*Can you recall a person's testimony or a time in your own
life when God touched your heart in a profound way?
Would your story encourage others to live God's Way?
Please share your story today, won't you?
God could use it to change a person's life forever.*

For Writer's Guidelines, future titles, and submission
procedures, visit:
www.godswaybooks.com

Or send a postage-paid, self-addressed envelope to:
God's Way, Editorial
6528 E. 101st Street, Suite 416
Tulsa, Oklahoma 74133-6754

This and other titles in the *God's Way* series
are available from your local bookstore.

God's Way for Couples
God's Way for Fathers
God's Way for Graduates
God's Way for Mothers
God's Way for Teens
God's Way for Women

Visit our website at:
www.whitestonebooks.com

*"...To him who overcomes I will give some of the hidden manna to
eat. And I will give him a white stone,
and on the stone a new name written which
no one knows except him who receives it."*
REVELATION 2:17 NKJV

WHITE STONE BOOKS
LAKELAND, FLORIDA